Young...

2004 POETRY C...

ONCE UPON
A RHYME

IMAGINATION FOR
A NEW GENERATION

. . . The End Of The Line Vol IV
Edited by Kelly Oliver

 Young**Writers**

First published in Great Britain in 2005 by:
Young Writers
Remus House
Coltsfoot Drive
Peterborough
PE2 9JX
Telephone: 01733 890066
Website: www.youngwriters.co.uk

SB ISBN 1 84602 085 9

Foreword

Young Writers was established in 1991 and has been passionately devoted to the promotion of reading and writing in children and young adults ever since. The quest continues today. Young Writers remains as committed to engendering the fostering of burgeoning poetic and literary talent as ever.

This year's Young Writers competition has proven as vibrant and dynamic as ever and we are delighted to present a showcase of the best poetry from across the UK. Each poem has been carefully selected from a wealth of *Once Upon A Rhyme* entries before ultimately being published in this, our twelfth primary school poetry series.

Once again, we have been supremely impressed by the overall high quality of the entries we have received. The imagination, energy and creativity which has gone into each young writer's entry made choosing the best poems a challenging and often difficult but ultimately hugely rewarding task - the general high standard of the work submitted amply vindicating this opportunity to bring their poetry to a larger appreciative audience.

We sincerely hope you are pleased with our final selection and that you will enjoy *Once Upon A Rhyme . . . The End Of The Line Vol IV* for many years to come.

Contents

Chetwynde School, Barrow-in-Furness

Heather Watts (8)	21
Hannah Bell (10)	21
Joseph Barton (10)	22
Emily Watts (10)	22
Amy Knowles (10)	23
Kathryn Cole (11)	23
Joshua James Spedding (8)	24
Amanda Marriott (10)	24
Jack Turner (8)	25
Lorna Sharpe (9)	25
Rosamund Bullard (9)	26
Jennifer Collings (9)	26
Anna Cooper (9)	26
Rebecca Wharton (8)	27

Elleray Preparatory School, Windermere

Imogen Hartley (8)	27
Matthew Harris (7)	27
Thomas Cliff (7)	28
Anna Broomby (8)	28
Isobel Barton (7)	28
Marcus Jepson (7)	29
Emma-Leigh Cooksey (8)	29
Eve-Elodie Metcalfe (7)	29
Harriet French (7)	30
Holly Southern (7)	30
Naomi Sanderson (7)	30
Oliver Kirk (8)	31
Matthew Jackman (8)	31
Mary Garrett (8)	32
Ben Gale (7)	32
Madeleine Sidi (8)	33
Jack Affleck (7)	33
Emily Howarth (8)	34
Bethan Cogger (7)	34
Matthew Jackman (9)	35
Jenny Claire Broomby (9)	35
Adam Scowcroft (8)	36
Alice Chadwick (9)	36
Samantha Asher (8)	37

Hayton CE Primary School, Brampton

Liam Michael Holliday (8)	57
Rachel Goodwin (9)	58
Charlotte Coombe (9)	58
William Gibson (8)	59
Joshua Pratt (8)	59
Ella Braidwood (10)	60
Christopher Brown (7)	60
Kirsty Norwood (10)	61
Rory Spencer (10)	61
Sarah Louise Wright (10)	62
Bradley Fisher (10)	62
Georgina Holmes (9)	63
Matthew Hogg (10)	63
Annika Davidson (10)	64
Matthew Smith (10)	64
Catherine Barr (10)	65
Alison Dunning (10)	65

Irthington Village School, Carlisle

Jesse Gray (10)	66
Ophelia Gia Appleby (8)	66
Ellie Gray (7)	67
Andrew Bryant (7)	67
Orlando Appleby (10)	68
Lachlan Ewart (7)	68
Oliver Barnes (9)	69
Emma Gallagher (8)	69
Joe Batey (10)	70
Rebecca Louise Grice (8)	70
Nina Russell (10)	71
Ellen Hill (7)	71
Philippa Bryant (9)	72
Amy Greenup (10)	73

Kingsbury Junior School, Kingsbury

Naomi Grace Guzder (7)	73

Kirkby Stephen Primary School, Kirkby Stephen

Group Entry Year 5 Lee McWhirter, Robert Keefe, Ryan Cooper, John Redmond, Thomas Dixon, Vicki Tunstall (9), Megan Bainbridge (10), Jake Bell & David Bowman   74

Group Entry Year 4 Jonathan Mells, Elliot O'Connor Ramsey, Sean Winder, James Birkbeck & Duncan Brunskill (8)   75

Lessness Heath Primary School, Belvedere

Connor Brownfield (9)	75
Ryan Church (9)	76
Neelam Sahota (9)	76
Grace Sheridan (9)	77
April Chapman (9)	77
Stacey Tuffin (9)	78
Reece Kidman (9)	78
Tosin Taiwo (9)	79
Rosie Bayne (10)	79
Toni-Louise Ciplinski (9)	80
Lucy Taylor-Pease (10)	80
Rhiana Hill (9)	81
Adam Harris (9)	81
Celine Dinning (9)	82
Adam Stacey (9)	82
Matthew Wishart (11)	83
Casey Finch (9)	83
Holly Sturgeon (9)	84
Jack Taylor (9)	84
Joshua Desmond (9)	84
Matthew Lanning (9)	85

Moretonhampstead Primary School, Newton Abbot

Frankie Stockford (9)	85
Josie Garland (9)	85
Cara Grimwade (10)	86

Potters Green School, Coventry

Hannah Watson (10)	86
Shannon Finan (10)	86
Cheryl Culliford-Whyte (10)	87
Amanda Bale (10)	87

Megan Morris (10)	87
Tamsin Collett-Cox (10)	88
Jodie Goodreid (10)	88
Iona win Channer (10)	88
Leah Davies (10)	89
Jenny Lambert (10)	89
Sean Hague (11)	89
Rosie Marsons (10)	90
Megan Judd (11)	90
Sophie Burgoyne (10)	90
Kayleigh Gray (11)	91
Jack O'Donnell (11)	91
Rebecca Oughton (10)	92
Demi-Lee Woods (10)	92
Jamie-Lisa Acton (10)	92
Charlotte Tyrrell (10)	93
Megan Mitchell (10)	93

Robert Ferguson Primary School, Carlisle

Sophie Gill (11)	93
Cara Forrester (11)	94
Joby Hodnett (10)	94
Emily Graham (10)	95
Katherine Bolton (10)	95
Thomas McMann (11)	96
Steven Atkinson (11)	96
Nicole Kidd (10)	97
Jamie Little (10)	97
Chloe Bell (10)	98
Deborah Harrop (11)	98
Adam Ramdin (10)	99
Anthony Heugh (10)	99
Lauren Lewis (10)	100
Natasha Isaacs (11)	100
Lucy Maxwell (10)	101
Jodie Liddell (10)	101
Hollie Smith (10)	102
Adam Gill (10)	102
Nathan Thompson (10)	103
Amber Jenkins (10)	103
Andrew Bell (10)	104

Hannah Potts (10)	130
Victoria Baker (9)	131
Jonathan Pickup (10)	132
Arabella Stalker (9)	133
Dale Mounsey (9)	134
Sam Blackburn (10)	135

Stainton CE Primary School, Penrith

Zoë Eland (8)	135
Emily Dunn (8)	136
Deza Thompson (8)	136
Katie Scott (8)	137
Elizabeth Richardson (8)	137
Bethany Rouse (8)	138
Lewis Pamphilon (8)	138
Georgina Fisher (8)	139
Jamie Leah (8)	139
Amy Hullock (8)	140
Greg Hall (9)	140
Tom Kendal (8)	140
Holly Foster (8)	141
Katy Mason (8)	141
James Buck (8)	141
Lucy Ward (8)	142
Ben Harvey (8)	142

The Poems

Thunderstorm

Crash, bash, thunder goes
Noise is all it makes.
Lightning strikes, thunder roars
And people go indoors.
Lightning stops, thunder growls
Lightning strikes again.
More and more it crashes and bashes.
Even more it thunders.
Thunder days, dark days, sometimes
Very thundery days.
More and more it thunders
More and more it rains.
Then the sun comes out
And we all go out to play.

Sophie Owen (10)

It's Snowing

It's snowing, it's snowing, what a wonderful day,
It's snowing, it's snowing, come and play.
The snow is falling on the trees,
It's so deep it's past my knees.
I build a snowman big and tall,
It makes me look very small.
The next day when I get up,
I find the snow has gone and the flowers have come.

Brandon Moffat

My Hopes And Dreams For The Future

I dream of no wars, but peace and love,
I dream of angels coming from above.
I dream of enjoyment, in everything we do,
I dream of hope for me and you.

I hope that we all fulfil our dreams,
I hope that illnesses won't be as bad as they seem.
I hope that in times of anger and stress,
I hope that sadness will become lesser and less.

I dream of all people to stand hand in hand,
Together we will build a better land.
I hope that the world will become fair, too,
I hope that all dreams will be granted true!

Sarah Roden (10)

Friends

Everyone needs someone to play with,
Everyone needs someone to care,
Everyone needs a very kind friend,
So you don't need to keep jumping in the air.

Yvette Agyekumhene (8)

The Weeping Willow

The master of beauty
The mistress of disguise
The beauty of the reflection
Blinds my eyes.

Rachel Ledner (9)

Night

Moles digging in the ground
Children spinning around
Wind blowing the blossom trees
Touching the frosty leaves
Jack Frost on my nose
Me wrapped up in layers of clothes
Dad drinking from a steaming cup
Seeing lights, lighting up
Twinkling stars in the night sky
Snow falling from way up high
Time for home
Time for bed
To lie down my sleepy head
Night, night, sleep tight
See you in the morning light.

Heather Longshaw (9)
Carmountside Primary School, Stoke-on-Trent

Night

Mice squeaking looking for food
Owls speaking in a mood
Foxes howling looking for bins
Rats scratching in tins
Children tasting the cold air
There's me, feeling a bit scared
Smelling petrol off smelly cars
Seeing beer in public bars
Touching frosty, rotten leaves
Hearing wind blowing trees
Time to go home
Time to go to bed
Time to dream with a sleepy head.

Rachel Diskin (8)
Carmountside Primary School, Stoke-on-Trent

Night

Mice squeaking looking for food
Dogs barking in a mood
Owls hooting while sitting up in a tree
Foxes are out going to bite me
In the sky at night
Little stars twinkle nice and bright
I can taste the damp, cold air
With the breeze running through my hair
The cities are quiet and the people lie still
Not a sound to be heard at the top of the hill
The rustling of the leaves at the bottom of my feet
The cold air turns to snow and sleet
My eyes are getting sleepy and it's time to go to bed
And wake up in the morning with a happy head.

Cherelle Jolley (9)
Carmountside Primary School, Stoke-on-Trent

My Pets

My dog is as soft as a polar bear
In snow.
And my dog is hungry as a
Crocodile in water.
My cat is furry as a mat and it has a
Nap.
And my cat likes chocolate ice cream more
Than white ice cream.

Dean Stephenson (9)
Castle Park School, Kendal

My Family

My mum is
cuddly and
my dad is
kind
my grandad is
very funny and
my grandma is
warm-hearted
my brother is
quite annoying and
my sisters are
very girly
Joelle is
cheerful and
Lauren is
a bit moody
Natalie is
bossy and
my nieces and nephews are
very cheeky
my cousins are
nice and great to be with
my aunties are
happy and
my uncles
get a bit stressed
and my friends
are the best
so I love my family all that much.

Sian Wightman (9)
Castle Park School, Kendal

The Bionic Booger

As I was walking
I sneezed and oh my,
How that booger began to fly.

It flew and it flew and it landed with a *splat!*
As if it was a falling acrobat.
When it began to ooze down, slowly,
It landed in an experiment at the local laboratory.

It grew gigantic to the size of a house
And made me feel like a helpless dormouse.
And slowly as it began to digest the city,
I tried to think of a way to destroy it quickly.

Then it hit me like a blow to the head,
Kill it like a cold of a kid in bed.
So as fast as I could, though speeding is a crime
I sped to the nearest tissue factory
And made them work double time.

They worked and they worked
At a feverish speed, to wipe the city clean.
It took all day, it took all night,
But the tissue was made and we were ready to fight.

We wiped up the phlegm.
We wiped up the green.
We wiped all day long
And we made the city gleam.

Gareth Baker (10)
Castle Park School, Kendal

Octopus

Octopus, octopus
big, slimy
octopus,
with eight big suckers,
sucking everything in its way.

Octopus, octopus
as big as a bulldozer,
always hiding, waiting for the right time to strike
its prey.

Octopus, octopus
as fast as fast can be
always flying through the sea.

Octopus, octopus
as rich as the Queen
with pearls and rubies all hidden
where no one will find them
in the sea.

Blake Wilson (10)
Castle Park School, Kendal

Supply Teachers

When I went into school one day
We had a phone call
Just to say,
That our teacher was taken sick
So instead, we had a
Supply called, Mr Hick,
He had dark hair and deep green eyes
Like evil emeralds in disguise,
He got the register out and said,
'Good morning Lucy and good morning Ned.'
Whilst we had to write millions of lines
He was just sitting there, reading The Times.

Gemma Burns (10)
Castle Park School, Kendal

Move Your Feet To The Undersea Beat!

The sharks find fish de-lish,
The jellyfish move so gracefully
And so do the cuttlefish,
The octopuses so sly they
Never catch your eye,
Dolphins jumping round and round,
Making a weird clicking sound.

When we go snorkelling, it's really rather fun,
Sunbathing under the scorching summer sun,
There are some wonderful creatures
On land, including the crab who buries in the sand,
The puffins are colourful and bright,
But often, they have a fight.

People building sandcastles,
Finding shiny shells
And eating ice cream.

So, don't you forget to
Move your feet to the undersea beat!

Zoe Barrett (9)
Castle Park School, Kendal

Speedy

I love Gumball 3000
speedy cars
Chopper coppers
Catching you
Nicking you.

But I love speed
A Nissan Skiline
A Ford Mustang
All looking forwards
To the finish.

James Dent (10)
Castle Park School, Kendal

I Love Food

My name is Victoria
I am ten
I love food
Like eggs from a hen
I love burgers and chips
And sausage and bacon
They make me lick my lips.

I also love things
That are, oh, so very scrummy
Strawberry rock, chocolate bars and candy,
They are so yummy.

Pizza and jacket potatoes
Fill me up just fine
Topped off with toppings
Like prawns squirted with lime.

On days that are hot and very sunny
Vanilla ice cream drizzled with honey
Goes down such a treat
Whilst sitting in the garden
On my garden seat.

I also love milkshakes shaken and sandwiches with ham
And I can't resist most food like roast lamb
And what I'm trying to conclude
Is that I love food.

Victoria Thompson (10)
Castle Park School, Kendal

My Kitchen

My kitchen has . . .
A kettle that goes click.
A tap that drips.
A washing machine that whispers.
A toaster that goes pop.
A microwave that goes ping.
A plate that smashes.
A dishwasher that goes wish-wash.
A dryer that whizzes.
A chair that creaks.
A clock that ticks.
A fridge that goes zzz.
A freezer that goes mmm.
A sink that gurgles.
A bread bin that goes crash.
A cupboard door that goes creak.
A switch that clicks.
A table that wobbles.
A jar that can smash.
A bin that you put your rubbish in.

Emma Dixon (9)
Castle Park School, Kendal

The Double-Headed Dragon

His eyes are like emeralds
And his teeth are stones,
He roars with great passion
And he has the strongest bones.

He has horns hard as metal
And stripes long as trees,
His mouth is sticky and horrible
And he has a nose like bees.

His fingers are hard and long,
As thick as his dark grey nails
And as he trudges through the land,
He opens all the jails.

But when he gets tired,
He's very sleepy,
But when he wakes up,
He's horribly sneezy.

But if you make him angry,
You could have a dreaded curse
And if you do,
He could make your bones burst.

Steven Tremeer (9)
Castle Park School, Kendal

My Pony

I have a pony she lives in my mind,
Her name is Willow,
I think of her all night,
While lying on my pillow.

She runs in the field,
She sleeps in the stable,
She lays in the garden,
She nicks food off the table.

I have a pony she comes to school with me,
She's black and white,
Her saddle is red,
Her eyes are bright.

She leaps over jumps,
She swishes her tail,
She lies on her back,
She chews the mail.

I love my pony,
In my mind,
She lives forever,
Up in my mind.

William Herbert (10)
Castle Park School, Kendal

Puppies And Kittens

Puppies, puppies, puppies
Different types of puppies
Labradors, Jack Russells or mongrels
And lots, lots more
Different types of names
Macey, Buster or Danny
Or lots, lots more.

Kittens, kittens, kittens
Different types of kittens
Stray, tabby or black
Plus lots, lots more
Different types of names
Lucky, Bananas or Tiddles
Also lots, lots more.

Macey, Buster and Danny
Watch them play
Slinking about in a pile of leaves
Lucky, Banana and Tiddles
Look at them play
Chasing a little toy mouse
Puppies and kittens
They're so much fun.

Aimee Bennett (10)
Castle Park School, Kendal

My Feelings

I'm bored,
I'm bored,
I'm really, really bored,
I'm stuck inside,
There's nothing on telly,
It's raining outside,
I've lost one welly.

I'm happy,
I'm happy,
I'm really, really happy,
It's sunny outside,
I'm going on my bike,
I'm going to ride,
With my friend, Mike.

I'm sad,
I'm sad,
I'm really, really sad,
There's hailstones outside,
I've fallen off my bike
And I've really, really cried
And this I don't really like.

I'm scared,
I'm scared,
I'm really, really scared,
It's creepy outside,
I'm all in the dark,
There's nowhere to hide,
Tap, tap, tap on my shoulder,
Who's there?

Nicole Robinson (10)
Castle Park School, Kendal

My Bedroom

My bedroom has,
A comfy bed
To rest in.
My bedroom has,
A bright light
To see in the dark.
My bedroom has,
A mirror
To see myself in.
My bedroom has,
A creaky door
To go out of.
My bedroom has,
Light pink walls
That you can see at night.
My bedroom has,
Purple curtains
That blow when the window's open.
My bedroom has,
A telly
To watch on a weekend.
My bedroom has,
A squeaky wardrobe
To put lots of clothes in.
My bedroom has,
A CD player
To listen to while chilling.
Bedrooms are great!

Danielle Hayton-Swindle (9)
Castle Park School, Kendal

My Living Room

In my living room I have:
Lovely leather sofas,
With nice cream walls,
With a nice wooden mirror.

In my living room I have:
A lovely brown rug,
With nice baggy lines,
With nice fluffy parts.

In my living room I have:
Lovely wooden floor,
With a nice dark colour to it,
With a nice cream colour.

In my living room I have:
A lovely leather stool,
With a lot of comfort,
With nice wooden stands.

In my living room I have:
Lovely sparkly lights,
With a nice shimmer all day,
With a nice shade.

In my living room I have:
Lovely wooden blinds,
With a nice window sill,
With a nice coffee table,
My living room is *great*.

Courtney Telford (10)
Castle Park School, Kendal

Mealtimes

I love mealtimes

Snap, crackle, pop
Rice Krispies for breakfast.

Munch, munch, munch
Sandwiches for dinner.

Chew, chew, chew
Pork chops for tea.

Crunch, crunch, crunch
Toast for supper.

Mmm, tomorrow I will have . . .

Sizzle, sizzle, sizzle
Bacon for breakfast.

Yum, yum, yum
Crisps for dinner.

Chomp, chomp, chomp
Chips for tea.

Slurp, slurp, slurp
A cup of tea with my supper.

I love breakfast
I love dinner
I love tea
I love supper
I love mealtimes!

Bethany Moffatt (9)
Castle Park School, Kendal

My School Is Old

My school is like a big old box
It has hundreds of pupils holding it up
It's like a ragged old shoe
That's barely there.

My school is like a big old box
I never want to come here again
It's smelly, horrible
And it might collapse.

My school is like a big old box
It's been here for hundreds of years
It does not have five teachers
Why do I come here?

My school is like a big old box
I have seven years to go
I will probably suffocate.

My school is like a big old box
My friends think I am old-fashioned
My mum and dad force me to go here.

My school is like a big old box
And I can't
I won't be free
It's like a hobby.

My school, my school, my school
It's like a big old box.

Calum Wells (9)
Castle Park School, Kendal

My Flower

There's a flower in my room
And it's very pretty
It stands in my window
And it's a pity
Because no one can see it
Except for me
No one looks
Not even my family
I love my flower
It is blue
I love it so much
And I bet you would too.

It's delicate
And sweet
It's pretty
And neat
I go to bed
And it's sitting there
Every day it gets fed
Because I love my flower.

Amy Brown (10)
Castle Park School, Kendal

The Caravan Of Doom

We bought a caravan eight years ago,
A nineteen-fifties Santamo,
We still have it to this day
And how I wish it would go away.

The interior is like a mouldy sack,
Perched upon a toast rack,
The caravan is really rusty,
The door is like bread gone crusty.

The bathroom is really small
And has black mould on the wall,
The sink is quite yuck,
Because it is full of muck.

The caravan is disgusting,
I really think it is rusting,
Now you know that it is foul,
Please help me get rid of it, *now!*

Molly Atkinson (9)
Castle Park School, Kendal

A Monster Ate My School

When I went to school one day,
Something came, to my surprise.
A monster eating the school,
I couldn't believe my eyes.

The monster was heading for my class,
So I threw a piece of glass.
The monster turned around and said,
'Who threw that piece of glass at my head?'

The monster went to the head teacher's office
And gobbled up Miss Morris.
I jumped inside the monster's mouth
And grabbed her out, along with a shout.

Joel George (8)
Cathedral School of St Saviour & St Mary Ovene, London

Sounds

Can you hear the sound of the wind
Whistling loudly through the trees?
Leaves are falling thick and fast
Rustling as they blow in the breeze.

Autumn is coming, the weather's getting cold
I can hear the rain splashing on the ground
Making puddles on the path
And pattering loudly all around.

Now the sun is shining out
The birds are chirping in the trees,
We're on our skates on the road
Ouch! I've fallen and hurt my knees.

People are chatting in the street
I can hear a dog barking behind a door
And the radio is playing a lovely tune
As you listen you can hear more and more.

Heather Watts (8)
Chetwynde School, Barrow-in-Furness

The Dolphin

The dolphin,
Loves company.
Beautiful, strong, shiny.
Skims through the water
Like a rocket.
It makes me feel happy,
Like I always want to smile.
The dolphin.
It reminds us our life is beautiful.

Hannah Bell (10)
Chetwynde School, Barrow-in-Furness

Animal Antics

One wise walrus waggled his whiskers
Two terrifying tigers tied up their tails
Three thirsty thrushes thought through their thirst
Four flying fish flew fearlessly fast and forward
Five feathery pheasants photographed phenomenal phones
Six slippery snakes slithered slowly and slyly
Seven sick sea lions sadly squeaked and squawked
Eight enormous elephants ate eight enormous envelopes
Nine naughty newts gnashed nourishing nutrients
Ten teasing turtles tickled their teacher.

Joseph Barton (10)
Chetwynde School, Barrow-in-Furness

The Solar System

The solar system,
Nine planets in all,
Fascinating, round, coloured,
Like footballs in the sky,
Or oranges in a line,
It makes me feel in awe,
Like a child looking up at an Olympian,
The solar system,
It reminds me that only Earth has life.

Emily Watts (10)
Chetwynde School, Barrow-in-Furness

Animal Adventures

One wobbly walrus washed his whiskers
Two terrible toucans talked trash
Three talkative thrushes thought things through
Four frightened flies fled from four ferocious frogs
Five flying fish flew from five fishing rods
Six sick seagulls slept soundly
Seven silly seals swallowed some shells
Eight enormous elephants ate excessively
Nine naughty newts nibbled nastily
Ten tiny termites trembled in a tree.

Amy Knowles (10)
Chetwynde School, Barrow-in-Furness

The Fierce Tiger

The fierce tiger.
Endangered all around the world.
Stripy, beautiful, fast.
Like a lion hunting for food,
Like a fox roaming around.
I feel sad and scared at the same time.
Like a tiny field mouse.
The fierce tiger,
Reminds us how thoughtless we are.

Kathryn Cole (11)
Chetwynde School, Barrow-in-Furness

Sounds

(In memory of my treasured baby brother Bradley Isaac Spedding, Saturday 22nd January 2005)

I hear the birds tweeting
I hear the rain tapping
I hear a plane zooming
And my Xbox game's zapping.

The bang of the cat flap
The crash of the door
The swish of the washer
The creak of the floor.

The ping of the microwave
The whirr of the computer
The click of the kettle
The spring of the toaster.

Joshua James Spedding (8)
Chetwynde School, Barrow-in-Furness

Animals In Action

One wet walrus waggled his whiskers
Two tame turtles tickled their toes
Three thrilled thrushes thrashed through a thicket
Four feathered pheasants fluffed their feathers
Five furry ferrets fiddled with their feet
Six scaly swordfish sold their scales
Seven silly seals slapped their stomachs
Eight elegant elephants examined their ears
Nine noisy newts nuzzled their knuckles
Ten terrifying tigers twiddled their tongues.

Amanda Marriott (10)
Chetwynde School, Barrow-in-Furness

Sounds

The scraping of the chairs
The creaking of the stairs
The flushing of the chain
The chuffing of the train.

The ringing of the bell
The wind on the fell
The shuffling of the books
The footsteps of the crooks.

The quacking of the ducks
The beeping of the trucks
The splatter of the rain
The take-off of a plane.

The key in the lock
The ticking of the clock
The popping of corns
The pipping of horns.

Jack Turner (8)
Chetwynde School, Barrow-in-Furness

Yellow

Yellow is for cats' eyes, lurking round the streets
Yellow is the colour of daffodils blooming
Yellow is the colour of stars glowing in the night
Yellow is the colour of the shining sun
Yellow is the colour of a ferocious lion
Yellow is for lemons growing on a tree.

Lorna Sharpe (9)
Chetwynde School, Barrow-in-Furness

Yellow

Yellow is honey running off a spoon
Yellow is a melon as round as the moon
Yellow is the sun beaming on the sea
Yellow is a stripe on the body of a bee
Yellow is as fluffy as a chick
Yellow is an ice lolly melting off a stick.

Rosamund Bullard (9)
Chetwynde School, Barrow-in-Furness

White

White is the paper on which we write
White is the toothpaste we use at night
White are the wisps in the sky above
White are the feathers of all the doves
White are the clouds that the north wind will blow
But my favourite white is fluffy white snow.

Jennifer Collings (9)
Chetwynde School, Barrow-in-Furness

Green

G rass does grow
R ising slow
E very day
E xcept in snow
N ature's way!

Anna Cooper (9)
Chetwynde School, Barrow-in-Furness

Sounds

The alarm clock rings to wake me up
The kettle bubbling to fill my cup
The shower tinkles in the bath
It really wants to make me laugh
The door bangs closed
The car moves fast
I get to school, 'Hooray!
Phew! I'm not the last!'

Rebecca Wharton (8)
Chetwynde School, Barrow-in-Furness

Tomato Pasta

A piece of pasta is like a telescope
With a pirate looking through it.
It feels like a worm
It tastes like a sunset
It smells like an Italian restaurant
It looks like a slug
It sounds like a silent wind
It reminds me of my mummy.

Imogen Hartley (8)
Elleray Preparatory School, Windermere

A Strawberry Milkshake

A milkshake is like a popping mixture.
It feels like a pink lake.
It tastes like a crushed strawberry.
It smells like France.
It looks like heaven.
It sounds like still bubbles.
It reminds me of my cousin, Chris.

Matthew Harris (7)
Elleray Preparatory School, Windermere

I Like Pizza

A pizza looks like a pyramid
Put together with cheese.
My favourite is ham and mushroom.
I even like the crust.
It sounds like a crunchy leaf.
It feels like a squidgy, hot slug.
It smells like an Italian restaurant.
It tastes like a dead mushroom
And it reminds me of my grandad.

Thomas Cliff (7)
Elleray Preparatory School, Windermere

My Food Poem

A milkshake is like a white hill covered in clouds.
It feels like cold snow.
It tastes like sugar.
It smells like fresh strawberries.
It looks like a bump on someone's head.
It sounds like sloppy mud.
It reminds me of my mum and dad.

Anna Broomby (8)
Elleray Preparatory School, Windermere

My Favourite Food

An ice cream is like a bald man's head
With a bug on top.
It smells like a box of expensive chocolates.
It tastes like an ice pack.
It looks like a mountain.
It sounds like falling jelly.
It reminds me of sheep.

Isobel Barton (7)
Elleray Preparatory School, Windermere

Sausages

A sausage is like a finger,
it feels like a rock that is bumpy,
it looks like a sausage dog,
it sounds like a plane crashing,
it tastes like orange juice,
it smells like pig,
it reminds me of my aunt's puppy.

Marcus Jepson (7)
Elleray Preparatory School, Windermere

My Food Poem

A fried sausage is like a skinny pig.
It feels like an autumn leaf.
It tastes like a bone.
It smells like a sheep.
It looks like an arm.
It sounds like a snake slithering.
It reminds me of my kitchen.

Emma-Leigh Cooksey (8)
Elleray Preparatory School, Windermere

Chocolate Bar

It feels like chocolate blood.
It tastes like chocolate sauce.
It smells like the lighthouse.
It looks like melted mud.
It sounds like the sun in the air.
It reminds me of angels and gods in the clouds.

Eve-Elodie Metcalfe (7)
Elleray Preparatory School, Windermere

A Spaghetti Bolognese

A spaghetti Bolognese is like a bowl of slimy slugs.
It feels like worms.
It tastes like early morning.
It smells like late at night.
It looks like it's scrumptious.
It sounds like snails slithering across the floor.
It reminds me of my back garden.

Harriet French (7)
Elleray Preparatory School, Windermere

My Favourite Food Is . . .

Chocolate.
A chocolate bar is like a board rubber.
It feels like a hard wall.
It tastes like a milkshake.
It smells sweet when you put it in your mouth.
It looks like a brick in a wall.
It sounds like a slug that is all still.
It reminds me of my mum.

Holly Southern (7)
Elleray Preparatory School, Windermere

Hot Chocolate

A hot chocolate is like a sea of coffee
With some boats floating.
It feels like cream,
It smells like melted chocolate.

It looks like an ocean,
It sounds like a pencil staying still,
It reminds me of a lake.

Naomi Sanderson (7)
Elleray Preparatory School, Windermere

Oliver Special

Ingredients
Chocolate cakes
33 armies
3 Crunchies
Weapons and armour
2 smiles
3g of cheekiness

How to make Oliver
Add 2 chocolate cakes
Blend 33 armies
Break 3 Crunchies into small pieces.
Slice weapons and armour
Put in oven for 10 minutes.
Whilst cooking, sprinkle 2 smiles and 3g of cheekiness
And out comes Oliver.

Oliver Kirk (8)
Elleray Preparatory School, Windermere

Misty Mountain

In the mist of a misty mountain
In the fog of a foggy fell
There is something quite fantastic
Something so dramatic!
Just come inside
And express your mind.

Beyond a mighty boulder
Past the flowing streams
Take no time to memorise
Just discover what's inside.

Something in your dreams you'll find
When you go round the corner you'll see what's inside.

Matthew Jackman (8)
Elleray Preparatory School, Windermere

Recipe For Mary

Ingredients
1 teaspoon of fun
2 handfuls of shyness
1 plate of helmets
1 pair of shorts
100 friends
7 helpings of sticky toffee pudding
100g of McFlurry
1 handful of pasta
2 pink lips
1 pair of brown eyes

Method
Break the fun into tiny pieces.
Mix well.
Sprinkle shyness into the bowl.
Add 7 helpings of sticky toffee pudding.
Stir well.
Pour 1 pair of pink lips into the mixture.
Heat the helmets up for approximately 15 minutes.
Now add 100 friends.
Grate over 1 pair of shorts.
Whisk 100g of McFlurry.
Drop in 1 handful of pasta and a pair of brown eyes.

Mary Garrett (8)
Elleray Preparatory School, Windermere

Ice Cream

My ice cream looks like a fish
Jumping out of the water.
The sauce looks like scales,
It feels like a snail,
It sounds like a slug.
It smells like a bunch of strawberries
And it reminds me of a mountain,
Covered in snow.

Ben Gale (7)
Elleray Preparatory School, Windermere

Recipe For Maddy

Ingredients
400g sticky toffee pudding
1 pair of riding boots
14 pieces of long brown hair
2 pairs of rabbit ears
9 pairs of horseshoes
500g of laughter

Method
Put in 400g of sticky toffee pudding.
Then drop in 1 pair of riding boots.
Mix 14 pieces of brown long hair.
Whisk for about 5 minutes.
After, throw in 2 pairs of rabbit ears.
Next, add 9 pairs of horseshoes.
Finally, sprinkle on 500g of laughter.
Bake for about 15 minutes
And out comes Madeleine Sidi.

Madeleine Sidi (8)
Elleray Preparatory School, Windermere

Banana Cake

I *love* banana cake
my mum always gives me some
to take to school.
One night
I woke up
and I just thought about
banana cake!
I crept downstairs . . .
But my mum saw me . . .
and sent me back to bed.

Jack Affleck (7)
Elleray Preparatory School, Windermere

Recipe For Emily

1 handful of trees
50g of ropes
500g of pizza
A teaspoon of rosy cheeks
5 pairs of hazelnut eyes
1 handful of laughter
A box full of smiles
700g of fungus
1 box of magnets
700 pieces of brown hair.

Get out the pan.
Turn the stove on.
Add all the ingredients, except pizza and fungus.
Wait for 10 minutes.
Then add fungus and pizza.
Turn the stove off.
Pour it on your plate.

Emily Howarth (8)
Elleray Preparatory School, Windermere

Bricks

A chocolate bar is like a brick wall.
It feels like a chubby pencil.
It tastes like a Crunchie.
It smells like a sweet.
It looks like a brick.
It sounds like the wind in the sky.
It reminds me of my sister.

Bethan Cogger (7)
Elleray Preparatory School, Windermere

Matthew's Mess

10 pancakes
700g cheekiness
A litre of cold ice cream
125g of melted toffee
Jumpy, muddy football boots
Chocolate flakes
Swaying orange hair.

How to make it
First slap 10 thin pancakes into a pan.
Pour in 700g of cheekiness, mingled with 125g of melted toffee.
Add some jumpy, muddy football boots.
Blend a litre of cold ice cream.
Then sprinkle some chocolate flakes.
Stir in swaying orange hair.
Finally, put in the oven and bake on high.
After half an hour, remove and serve Matthew
Fresh to the table.

Matthew Jackman (9)
Elleray Preparatory School, Windermere

Funky Food Poem

Mum and I munch at the mouth-watering mango.
It mushes and melts in our mouths.

Slimy spaghetti slithers into my mouth
Turning soggy as it slaps about in my jaws.

Red-hot risotto rumbles round the red pan.
It wriggles around my tummy.

Peppery prawn pizza, peeling in the oven.
It pops, pings and prances like a pink panther.

Tinkling tuna tiptoes round the table.
Trying to topple over the toy tiger.

Jenny Claire Broomby (9)
Elleray Preparatory School, Windermere

Adam's Recipe

Ingredients
101 steaks
72 packets of crisps
2 million maggots
Juice of ten fishes
500 pairs of fishing gear
1000g of tuna and sweetcorn
10 pairs of football boots
1 million footballs
1 pair of blue eyes
1 CD of Slipknot

Method
Put in 101 steaks, then add 72 packets of crisp.
Blend in 2 million maggots, then pour the maggot juice into 10 fishes.
Sprinkle 500 pairs of fishing gear.
Add 1000g of tuna and sweetcorn put together.
Stir 10 pairs of football boots for 1 hour.
Add 1 CD of Slipknot.
Melt of pair of blue eyes, then pour into a bowl.
Add 1 million footballs, then put all of it in an oven for 24 hours.
Then you have done.

Adam Scowcroft (8)
Elleray Preparatory School, Windermere

Spaghetti

Slippery spaghetti swirling around like worms.
Slimy spaghetti making me squirm.
Steaming spaghetti slithering around my fork.
Stringy spaghetti on the plate with some pork.
Spicy spaghetti is always a nice treat.
Slithery spaghetti is very nice with meat.

Alice Chadwick (9)
Elleray Preparatory School, Windermere

Recipe For Me

500g fish
2 plates of cooked snails
15 plates of sausages
50 pheasants
5 strands of strawberry-blonde hair
2 blue eyes
5 teaspoons of smiley faces
Lots of kindness
A lot of friendliness
5kg of fun

Method
Take a large cooking bowl
Stir up 500g of fish with 2 plates of snails
Add the sausages and cook for 2 minutes
Add the pheasants.
Sprinkle 5 strands of strawberry-blonde hair.
Mix in 2 blue eyes.
Pour on 5 teaspoons of kindness and friendliness.
Put in 5kg of fun and lots of bird watching.
Bake for 10 minutes.
Out will come Samantha Anne Sipple Asher.

Samantha Asher (8)
Elleray Preparatory School, Windermere

Fishy Food

Sushi, sushi, sloppy sushi soaking around the dish.
Slushy sushi smelling, stinky sliding off the spoon.
Swordfish, swordfish sleeping dead.
Swordfish sharpening its sword, stiff.
Oily oysters opening their shells.
People peeking for a pearl.

Sam Barton (9)
Elleray Preparatory School, Windermere

Isaac Special

Ingredients
Obelisk the tormentor card
Slifer the sky dragon card
Winged dragon card
Plate full of chocolate
Yorkshire pudding
Pepperoni pizza
Wildness
Maggots
Busted CD

Binoculars Method
Put in Obelisk the tormentor.
Add Slifer the sky dragon.
Blend in the plate full of chocolate.
Then whisk in the winged dragon card.
Add the Yorkshire pudding, stir for ten minutes.
Add pepperoni pizza, with extra pepperoni.
Then a box of wildness.
Blend in a box of maggots,
A Busted CD,
Last of all, a pair of small binoculars.
Bake for two hours in a 150°c oven.
Out comes a chocolate cake of Isaac Rigby-Nelson.

Isaac Rigby-Nelson (8)
Elleray Preparatory School, Windermere

Simply Scrumptious

Simply soothing sausages sizzling in a saucepan.
Bubbling beans bouncing onto my plate.
Bananas behaving badly in the custard.
Ravenously ravaging risotto roaring in my mouth.
Slithering spaghetti squirming in my bowl.
Beautiful broccoli bathing in gravy.

Kate Whittenbury (9)
Elleray Preparatory School, Windermere

The Harriet Ducker Surprise

Ingredients
5 prawns
1 hairy riding whip
A pair of hazel eyes
A sprinkle of freakiness
10 small toes
800g of hamster whiskers
2 plates of horseshoes
10 chilli and pepperoni crisps

Break 10 chilli and pepperoni crisps into little pieces.
Melt 1 plate of horseshoes and put the other plate to the side.
Grate 5 prawns into the crisps and mix them together.
Pour in the melted plate of horseshoes.
Add 10 small toes, a sprinkle of freakiness,
A hairy riding whip and a pair of hazel eyes.
Now blend them all together.
Throw in 800g of hamster whiskers.

And out comes a Harriet Ducker surprise.

Harriet Ducker (8)
Elleray Preparatory School, Windermere

My Special Spaghetti

My mum cooks me spaghetti as a special supper wish.
Its scrumptious smell makes me smile.
The garlic bread, it's a supper supreme.
But as much as I try, I never clear the dish.
It slips, it slides, it slithers around.
With my smooth silver spoon, I scoop and I scoop.
And I start to succeed!
Until my special spaghetti
Begins to make me leave.

James Kirkpatrick (9)
Elleray Preparatory School, Windermere

Recipe For Me

Ingredients
1 large plate of chocolate cake
3 big smiles
A handful of cheekiness
10 long brown hairs
2 pairs of jodhpurs
1 whip and hat
2 small ponies
Saddle and bridle
800g of sweets
200g of rusty horseshoes

How to make
Take one *big* bowl.
Tip in the large plate of chocolate cake.
Pour in the saddle and bridle.
Whisk vigorously for 1 minute.
Carefully stir in the cheekiness a drop at a time.
Grate the rusty horseshoes and fold them in with a wooden spoon.
Gently blend in the sweets, sprinkle in the 2 ponies
And jodhpurs and stir for 2 minutes.
After stirring, add the well-used crop and hat,
Then whisk in the 3 big smiles with the long brown hair.
Heat in the oven for 10 seconds and you will find me,
Elisabeth Bolger.

Elisabeth Bolger (8)
Elleray Preparatory School, Windermere

Food Poem

A luscious lemon lying like a lovely leopard on a lawn.
The prickly pineapple perched precariously on a palm tree.
The gorgeous green grapes grew gradually upon a great grapevine.
The mouth-watering melons melted in my bowl.
The burned bhaji was boiling badly.
The stringy spaghetti was sizzling sensationally.

John Clifford (9)
Elleray Preparatory School, Windermere

The Georgina Rose Surprise

Ingredients
12 rusty horseshoes
1 hairy riding whip
1 pair of bright blue eyes
900g melted chocolate
1 hour of cheekiness
900g of Yorkshire puddings
12 chilli and pepperoni crisps

Method
Break 12 chilli and pepperoni crisps into a big mixing bowl.
Whisk 12 rusty horseshoes into a bowl, melt and leave to one side.
Sprinkle 1 hairy riding whip over the top of the chilli and pepperoni crisps and stir in 900g of melted chocolate with the other ingredients.
Add the melted rusty horseshoes to everything.
Finally, stir in 900g of Yorkshire puddings and 1 hour of cheekiness.
Whisk for 5 minutes and then put in the oven at 200°c.
Leave for approximately 20 minutes.
When cooked, sprinkle 1 pair of bright blue eyes.
There you have Georgina Rose.

Georgina Rose (8)
Elleray Preparatory School, Windermere

Food Poem

Purple pepperoni pizza popping in a pink pan.
Spicy, spotty spaghetti swirling on a spoon.
Red-raw risotto roasting on the roof.
Bubbling banana burning on the beach.
Kicking and killing kiwi in Kenya.
Tiny, titchy tomato tumbling down town.
Pink potato pieces playing on a plate.

Gabriella Freeman (9)
Elleray Preparatory School, Windermere

Fabulous Food

Crunchy chapatti with coiled crisps, crowned cautiously.
Swirly spaghetti spilling sauce on the spinning tureen.
Ravioli rapidly running to the ravenous mandible.
Magnificent, miraculous macaroni strikes into the jaw,
Gnawing, chomping the macaroni down the manoeuvring throat.
Romantic risotto mixed with ravaging rocket going down
The runny mouth.
Magnificent mango having moistening massages, marching merrily
On the sizzling-mad, sweltering pan.
Passionate pizza passing the pepperoni to the exploding,
Popping paella in a purple pan.
Deep fried crispy beef, Peking style in, a bobbing, boiling hot boiler.
Fillet steak, Cantonese style, sawing this way and that
In the sizzling, saucy, sour soup.
Canton chef special fried rice, frying to and fro from the fizzing
And foaming, damp, cold plate.
Jumbo mussels with chilli sauce, eaten by munching
Mini max on March.
Prawn crackers crunching, chomping, curling cautiously
Into the giant mouth.

Jacky Keung (9)
Elleray Preparatory School, Windermere

Lovely Food Poem

Swirling spaghetti on the stove,
Squiggling, slopping and slouching around.

Perfect pizza in the pan,
Pancetta, peas and Parma ham.

Mushy macaroni in my mouth,
Mashed with mozzarella, meat and mango.

Revolting risotto rumbling in tummies,
Rolling and wriggling round.

Bendy, bouncy bananas,
Big and bursting on the barbecue.

Chloe Sammons (9)
Elleray Preparatory School, Windermere

A Food Poem

Mouth-watering mango
melting in my mouth.

Munchy macaroni
melting in my mouth.

Crunchy chapattis
crumbling as I crunch.

BBQ bananas being
brought for brunch.

Swirling spaghetti
spoiling Sam's supper.

Claire Fletcher (9)
Elleray Preparatory School, Windermere

Chickens

The chickens
Never go in at night.
Then, just that night the fox comes,
It snares around the ark,
The chickens peck away at the wood
And then we awake,
We see the fox attacking the chickens,
But one has to die.
It's the one that is the slave
And then the fox runs off
With the chicken in its mouth
And now the farmer's hunting,
Hunting for the one fox.

Jack Whittaker (9)
Hayton CE Primary School, Brampton

Black And White World

Grey sky, black clouds, white field
Full of dullness and despair.

The silence of the cold world
Creeps into another's pearly eye
To fill with grey tears
And trickle down a lonely face.

But in the end a mournful smile
Breaks through the tears.
There's no happiness in a cruel,
Harsh place like this.

You will become a traitor in this world.
Our world.
Your world.
Nobody's world.
A black and white world.

But the captivating beauty
Seeps through the unhappiness
Of a black and white world.

Our black and white world.
But there is good in our world.

Georgia Robinson (8)
Hayton CE Primary School, Brampton

Winter Nights

W inter nights are chilly and cold.
 I cicles are hanging from the roof, making a noise to music.
 N ippy it is, outside the snow is really deep.
 T ip of the snowman's nose is an ice cube as long as a hose.
 E xtra cold it is outside, but inside it is lovely and warm.
 R eally cold and really gusty it is outside.

Elliott Baines (7)
Hayton CE Primary School, Brampton

World War II

Bombs dropping,
Planes flying
Guns shooting
It's World War II!

Trenches are full as British kill,
Germans worry as England bomb,
Everybody's in their cellars, waiting for that moment.
Germans think they've won, but it's still going on.

It's night-time, but people are still alert.
This is the worst time of the night,
Britain could strike any minute,
A cry rings out, 'They're here!'

Everybody rushes to their cellars
As Britain destroys Berlin.
An oil factory blows up, killing thousands.
There's nothing Germany can do.

The war is over now,
The world
Is at peace
Britain won the war!

Fergus Spencer (8)
Hayton CE Primary School, Brampton

Winter Nights

W inter nights with the breezy cold
 I cy snowflakes like glittering stars
N orth wind is coming to freeze us
T he icicle points are making themselves
E ntertainment with the fireworks
R ather be inside by the blazing fire.

Christian Davidson (8)
Hayton CE Primary School, Brampton

My Pets

Running round like hurricanes,
But still warm when they stop,
Tripping me up to give me sprains,
Tiring me out to make me flop.

Giving me a lick,
To make me sick,
Causing more trouble than the house,
But still scared of a woodlouse.

Jumping out at cars,
Amazed by the stars,
They love walks,
But are frightened by the hawks.

Spraying their food everywhere,
Pouncing on each other, unaware,
Dripping water all over the floor,
They are always wanting more.

Fighting when we start to eat,
Barking at sheep, making them bleat,
Dogs are the best,
Even though they are pests.

Katie Hammond (8)
Hayton CE Primary School, Brampton

Winter Nights

W inter nights are nippy, chilly and freezing cold
 I ce shining dull and dark, sparkling tiny stars
N orth wind's in the sky, playing with the snow
 T ips of icicles growing bigger and bigger, making snowmen fall
E very child tries to make one, but they just fall down.
R ound snowflakes falling from the sky, they will make you
                                        freezing cold.

Alex Forster (7)
Hayton CE Primary School, Brampton

Time

It never seems to wait for you,
Always rushing ahead, shouting, 'Come on!'
But you can't catch up, you're 'behind the times'.
But if you stop, you lose your youth and grow taller,
Fatter, wrinkly, slower.
Someday you have to stop,
Otherwise your brand new shoes get worn out,
Or the whole world soon shrivels up
And dies and you are left standing,
Running after time
With no friends, like a fool.

Soon your emotions get the better of you
And you fall, dead.
Gone with your friends, murdered by time.
Once you have gone, that is when time dies.
When the clock strikes thirteen.
Time just blows up, *boom!* Just like that.
You are a hero, you have destroyed time.

Annie Young (8)
Hayton CE Primary School, Brampton

Winter

W inter nights are freezing cold
 I cy snowflakes fall
N o one knows when it will stop falling
 T -shirts are for summer so we do not put them on
 E specially when it is really cold
 R olling down the hill faster and faster.

Alexandra Howard (7)
Hayton CE Primary School, Brampton

Long Ship

It slides through the water
With its bank of bristling oars,
Raiding all the monasteries
Raiding the treasure floors.

The monks all flee
As the Vikings raid
The history of Scandinavia
Has been made.

Now to battle,
Now to die,
The air is filled
With shouts and a cry.

Lots of farming,
Lots of wheat,
Lots of new people
To make friends with and meet.

Now to home
With the history of the Vikings made.

Stuart Astle (8)
Hayton CE Primary School, Brampton

Winter

W inter nights will rule the Earth
 I n you run to the burning fire
N ippy air outside the door
 T he snow drifts down on the roof
E xit here outside we go
R un and run, then stop and smell the winter air.

Emma Cairns (7)
Hayton CE Primary School, Brampton

School Is Like A Prison

School is like a prison.
All sweaty and hard working.
Nowhere to escape.

We go out for an hour
And play out on the grass.
We come straight back in
And go back into class.

Then you paint some pictures
And the day is nearly over.
When the end of the day bell goes
It's like winning the World Cup.

When you see your parents in the car park
It's an even better thought.

Dominic William Simpson (9)
Hayton CE Primary School, Brampton

Winter Night

W inter's night brings the frosty wind scratching on your windows
          The falling snowflakes come down
 I n December when the snow comes faster and faster
          Leaves fall and the grass goes wet
N overmber brings the frost
          And the nippy nights
T ries to bite me, nippy night
          Or my feet will freeze
E at warm chocolate in the dark, frosty night
          Come to see if the boys and girls are asleep
R ain falls and snow comes
          But something happens at night.

Ashleigh Backhouse (7)
Hayton CE Primary School, Brampton

Knight

Their armour is thick and cold.
Their swords are sharp and fearless.
And their shields are steel and hard.
Their spears are sharp and long.

Their bows are wooden and long.
And their axes are sharp and heavy.

Do you want to be a knight?

The misty earth is around them.
While they go to war.
And the rain starts going cold as it goes on.
The ruins on the fortress will soon fall.

The gate has been broken and men might fall,
Their death is soon coming.
Now we must not flee or the fortress will be theirs.

Well, now get their king, but we'll fall.
Now our captain is dead . . .
Flee!
But they still chase us and there are only ten men left.

Max Sharp (8)
Hayton CE Primary School, Brampton

Winter

W inter is icy and cold
 I nside is cosy and warm and there is a lovely fire
N ippy, cold, icy, frosty, snowy snowflakes outside
T ingling fingers in front of the fire
E normous piles of snow outside that children will kick around
R ough snow, tidy snow, deep as a snowstorm.

Emily Bell (7)
Hayton CE Primary School, Brampton

Man U Groove

Giggs down the line to Rooney who sits on the ball then says,
'I have to go off the field.' And asks for his inhaler and goes back on.
Ferdinand asks, 'What's going on?'
'He needed his inhaler so that's why he went off.'
Giggs goes down the line, passes to the goal. What a goal!
Fletcher asks Kleberson, 'Why did you get a yellow card?'
'Because I said, *'Ow!'*'
The ref gives Neville a red and hits him twice on the head.
The ball gives its all.
So does Man U.
The red shirts have the ball. What a goal!
The ref goes on the sideline to go and have a look.
The ref puts them in the book.
Nistelrooy to Rooney to Bellion
To Giggs on the end of the ball, bends.
Time has gone, have a scone.

Adam Matthew Roberts (8)
Hayton CE Primary School, Brampton

Winter

W inter is freezing cold
 I am sitting next to the blazing fire to keep warm
N othing like shining frost
 T he glittering snow falling from the sky
 E ating my toast and drinking my chocolate
 R ing the bell, ready for bed.

Emily Henderson (7)
Hayton CE Primary School, Brampton

Monkey

Roaming in the wild,
With spices they taste mild.
Sometimes they get put in a cage,
They also go on stage.
Jumping from tree to tree,
Swinging wild and free.
Howling very loud,
Looking very proud.
We should let these creatures be,
Roaming joyful and free.
Grooming each other,
Suckling from their mother.
Using leaves as cover
And precious to a nature lover.
These creatures might get stuffed,
But we should get their fur fluffed.

Joel Daniel Braidwood (9)
Hayton CE Primary School, Brampton

Winter

W hizzing winter flying in the sky
 I cy ponds, ducks skating
N ibbling cookies, drinking hot chocolate
T he tip of the snowman's nose is frozen
E verywhere people are snug in their beds
R aindrops in the sky, children are playing in the snow.

Marcus Alastair Barnes-Batty (9)
Hayton CE Primary School, Brampton

The Journey

I went on a journey
And the flies rattled on my window.
The dogs in the boot
Barked in the car.

I ate sweets on the journey,
I saw four windmills,
Some cows,
A horse and sheep.

My mum was driving
And my dad was asleep.
I was squealing in the car
And I woke my dad up
And I went to sleep.

Natalie Hill (8)
Hayton CE Primary School, Brampton

What I Wish

I wish my school had a swimming pool
With a cool ride that's a slide.
I wish I could fly so high
I could touch the sky.
I wish I had a bear with lots of hair.
I wish people would never lie.
I wish people never cried
And that is what I wish.

Wayne Coulthard (9)
Hayton CE Primary School, Brampton

Viking Attack

Lindisfarne monks,
Praying and singing,
As the church bells are ringing.
Viking long ships
Come to the coast,
Treasures and riches
Expecting the most.
In the name of Thor's hammer,
Shield and swords clammer.
Block, block and strike,
Down fall the monks
At the edge of a pike.
Blood all a-splatter,
All is the matter.
The blood has been shed,
Now all are dead.
The story is done
And so are the monks.

Liam Ogden (11)
Hayton CE Primary School, Brampton

Moving On

Crunching leaves beneath my feet,
The autumn sound of whispering teeth,
Walk back home with crisp, white toes,
Tripping over the snow-white hose.

You pick yourself up whilst brushing off the snow,
Open the door and look at the glow,
The snow smashes on the glass,
Creeps in the corner and freezes the brass.

Rachael Holden (10)
Hayton CE Primary School, Brampton

Winter Nights

W inter wind swirling and twirling about in the air
 I n the house we're having marshmallows and drinking hot chocolate
N orth wind snowflakes shining like stars on the ground
 T he sleet is falling, when it hits the ground it goes *splosh!*
E ating the boiling hot chicken is lovely
R eally cold snow gusting about. My snowman has got blown over.

Daniel Kirk (8)
Hayton CE Primary School, Brampton

Winter Nights

W inter nights cosy and snug by the roaring fire
 I ce and frost scratching at the windows
N ippy wind blowing loose branches off trees
 T rees rustling, snowmen getting bigger and bigger every day
E specially snug in bed, wrapped in a cosy quilt
R aving cold where the snowmen are every year.

James Norwood (7)
Hayton CE Primary School, Brampton

Winter Days

W inter days are sparkly and bright, with frost all over the ground
 I love sitting by the fire drinking cocoa, *mmm*
N ow it is Christmas Eve and it is time to go to bed
 T omorrow it will be the big day
E very day I will play with these toys
R ed lights all over the Christmas tree.

Jessie M Dawson (7)
Hayton CE Primary School, Brampton

Slyness

He slinks out at night,
Out of a hole,
Into the darkness,
Then out of the darkness,
Into the farm.

He creeps to the door
Of the hen house,
Creaks it open
And springs!

Mayhem of feathers and dust,
Screams and squawks and howls!
A pecked fox, a chewed chicken,
A streak of red and white!

An angry shout, a deafening *bang!*
A howl of fright,
But a not hurt fox
Canters into the night.

Away he runs, away, away,
Back to the hole
Where his hungry children lie in wait.

Back, back, back to the forest,
Where his starving wife
Awaits his coming.

Winding through twists and turns,
Turning through the winds and twists,
The farmer pursues the fox
In the vague forest mist!

But at last, he reaches safety,
In the hole
Where he was born.

Miriam van den Berg (8)
Hayton CE Primary School, Brampton

The Zoo

There was a monkey
He was so funky
When he was locked in bars
He went to test driving a bus
But then he bought a car.

Here comes a pig
And with a fig
He thought it was nice
Before he had a bowl of rice
And it was made of mice.

There was a cow
He took a bow
In front of a crowd
That's the cow's first bow
In front of the entire crowd.

Here comes a tiger
With some bread
He went to bed and bumped his head
And then he met a chicken
Eating chicken legs.

The tiger gave him a fright
Then he drank Becks.
The chicken was drunk
He got in the funk
With the disco lights.

He turned on the music
And went boogie-woogie!
That's the end of that.

Liam Michael Holliday (8)
Hayton CE Primary School, Brampton

I Wish

I wish that school
Had a pool,
I wish I could fly
In the sky,
I wish school
Did not rule,
This is what I wish.
I wish I went on holiday
Every day.
I wish there were no bullies.
I wish that I could
Run fast.
This is what I wish
I wish I could
Talk to a fish.
I wish I could
Have magic.
I wish I could stop
The wind from blowing.
This is what I wish.

Rachel Goodwin (9)
Hayton CE Primary School, Brampton

Valentine

When I receive my Valentine's card
I first hesitate before opening it.
And when I do
I will get one of these sensations -
I will get very happy
Or very disappointed.

Charlotte Coombe (9)
Hayton CE Primary School, Brampton

You Have Put Me Off My Food

You know when you ate some worms
Thinking they were strings of cheese?
And what about the time you ate beetles
Thinking about beans?
Oh, I like to eat fish, chips, sauce and beans
And cheese strings.
They taste like proper food.

If my food was not nice,
I would be sick each day, oh yes.
Once you were eating fish
And I was being sick.
I just can't live with me being sick!

William Gibson (8)
Hayton CE Primary School, Brampton

Dirty Fields

In the dirty fields, there are little bugs
And animals like horses, cows and sheep
And the mud that pigs like playing in
All the time and everywhere
And horses running around the place.
Cows like eating grass
And they make a funny noise that sound like *moo!*
Sheep have a woolly coat all around them
To keep them warm in the winter.
In the summer, the farmer cuts their coats
So they don't get too hot.

Joshua Pratt (8)
Hayton CE Primary School, Brampton

A Scent Of Magic

The smell lingered all around me,
The smell of magic,
The aroma of magic,
No one can hear magic,
But magic still has thoughts,
Magic still has a will,
A scent,
A mind,
A brain,
Magic has been forgotten,
Left behind,
In the past,
But it's still there,
Still fighting to get out,
Out of a magical prison,
Where it was put,
Left,
Forgotten
And I know that because,
I am magic.

Ella Braidwood (10)
Hayton CE Primary School, Brampton

The Rabbit

Hear the rabbit,
Swiftly skipping,
Past the apples
And people picking.

Passing people,
One by one,
Picking apples,
Ton by ton.

Christopher Brown (7)
Hayton CE Primary School, Brampton

The Battle Of Lindisfarne

Monks working peacefully hour by hour,
Seeing the buds open flower by flower.
Working away in the heat of the sun,
Praying to God, praise Mighty One!

Suddenly a storm begins to rage,
People struggling from their old age.
Raging water splashes high,
High enough to reach the sky.

Suddenly a figure of a boat,
Silhouettes of people in black coats.
Hearing chants of Vikings strong,
In their boats very long.

Frighteningly the boats put in,
Vikings here of mighty sin.
The Vikings charge at the working monks,
Some still sleeping in their bunks.

Vikings are killing everyone,
Attacking monks singing a song.
Soon they begin to go back to their boat,
Hoping that it was still afloat.

Riding the sea which has now turned red,
From all the blood that has been shed.
Now the Vikings have gone home,
The monks can rebuild their monastery home.

Kirsty Norwood (10)
Hayton CE Primary School, Brampton

Big Bill

A farmer named Big Bill,
Was chucking out lots of pig swill,
When along came a tractor
And killed his friend Hector,
Before he had written his will.

Rory Spencer (10)
Hayton CE Primary School, Brampton

My Animals

I have ten animals
Two rabbits, Flopsy and Snowy,
Five guinea pigs, Speedy, Shy, Ant, Dec and Codey
Three birds, Fizz, Nemo and Midnight.

I look after them every day,
I clean them out every weekend,
I get them out every day,
I am so glad I've got them.

Ant, Dec and Codey are boys,
Speedy and Shy are girls,
Flopsy and Snowy are girls,
Fizz, Nemo and Midnight are boys.

I have had Flopsy four years,
I just got Snowy, Ant, Dec, Codey, Speedy and Shy,
I just got Midnight,
I already had Fizz and Nemo.

Sarah Louise Wright (10)
Hayton CE Primary School, Brampton

Poem Of Cakes

Fruit cakes, fairy cakes, cream cakes too,
Yummy and sweet
Creamy chocolate,
Spice, toffee, cherry and pineapple
Just for you.
Cakes are juicy, cakes are sweet
I have nothing else to eat.

Bradley Fisher (10)
Hayton CE Primary School, Brampton

Monks Death

Peacefully working
In the cold,
Digging,
Cooking,
Singing,
Praying,
Working hard.

Suddenly there's lightning
In the cloudy sky,
A Viking long ship,
Coming to attack,
In the storming sea,
The ship is coming closer.

On the land,
Bang!
Crash!
Fire burning,
Monks drowning in the sea
That's the end of that.

Georgina Holmes (9)
Hayton CE Primary School, Brampton

The Viking Attack On Lindisfarne

The Vikings came over in their long ships
Raging in terror and fear
Lindisfarne tremble in fear.
The Vikings hit Lindisfarne like a stone
Leaving a trail of bodies and blood behind them.
Sparing some for slaves.

Matthew Hogg (10)
Hayton CE Primary School, Brampton

The White Bengal Tigers

Roaming through the rainforest.
All that we can see.
Colours all around us.
Beautiful as can be.

If you listen carefully.
This is what you hear.
You hear the parrots sitting in the tree.
The songbirds very near.

Then we sniff the ground.
Sniffing for our prey.
Then there is a movement.
And we have caught our prey.

Padding through the jungle.
Feeling at the ground.
Silently we pad.
Soft and sharp things all around.

This is our life.
This is all it is.
No one can change me.
Not ever.

Annika Davidson (10)
Hayton CE Primary School, Brampton

Viking Long Ship

Rain crashed down
upon the ship,
as they sailed to Lindisfarne.
Viking berserkers
raided the shore,
killing all in their way.
They took some prisoners
and drowned the rest,
in the sea.

Matthew Smith (10)
Hayton CE Primary School, Brampton

Seasons

F irstly, there's spring
A quiet season,
S low and steady
T ired and tinted.

S easons and months
E nclosing at winter
A nd starting up in spring,
S ome minutes go by
O n the twelve-hour clock,
N ow it's ending, season's gone.

G oing by again and again
O ut and out till the season ends.

B ye, bye season, see you next year,
Y elling, 'Winter's here again.'

Catherine Barr (10)
Hayton CE Primary School, Brampton

Viking Invasion

In the distance
the monks can see a rocking ship
bobbing up and down in the sea.
They can hear chains,
they can hear shouting,
they can hear sails flapping in the wind
and swords being sharpened.
The monks are scared
but do not speak,
they run and hide in the monastery.
The Vikings have hit the land.
The monks can hear chains
clashing and hitting the walls,
the monks try to run
but the door opens.

Alison Dunning (10)
Hayton CE Primary School, Brampton

Heaven

The sky is blue
The sun is out too
My skin is healthy and fresh
The animals aren't locked behind wire mesh
The frogs jump and leap
At night we watch the tigers sleep.
I swim by the waterfall
Until I hear my mother call.
The smell of fresh fish lying in a dish
Makes my mouth water
After I go to my private quarter
In the morning we boat out
To catch my favourite . . . *trout!*
At night we go out to the lagoon
Where we swim and watch the moon.
The sky is blue
The grass is green
This is my heaven
So keep it a secret.
Shhhh!

Jesse Gray (10)
Irthington Village School, Carlisle

Katrina

Katrina is funny and strange
She makes up a drama club range
She's great and she's good
She plays Robin Hood
I hope that she'll never change
For if she did
I'd flip my lid
It would be a nightmare if she hid
But from now on, she'll never be gone
And that's how I'd like it to go on.

Ophelia Gia Appleby (8)
Irthington Village School, Carlisle

My Dog, Mazie

She's skinny and strong,
Two ears, a pointy nose,
She looks like a boy
Yes, she's my dog, Mazie.

She's greasy and furry,
With a very wet nose,
She's got short fur
And she's very funny.

She's soppier than my mum,
She's very fast
And very playful.

Four legs and funny,
She jumps like a deer.
Yes, that's my dog
Mazie Gray,
Who eats meat every day.

Ellie Gray (7)
Irthington Village School, Carlisle

They Are

Strong and rough as tough as a dinosaur
They can be small but very *scary*
Black, spiky, forked tongue, eating
They are prehistoric creatures
Living in today's world
Lounging like lions, they like eating small creatures
They are?
Komodo dragons.

Andrew Bryant (7)
Irthington Village School, Carlisle

Paradise

In this peaceful, perfect, pleasant place
Great cats roam freely;
Mango trees stretch out of the blue-green sea
And below the surface.
Cavernous caves of coral,
On land, massive veldts of gigantic ferns.
Magnificent trees hold tree villas;
Monkeys, gibbons, squirrels,
Chipmunks, bats,
Friendly snakes and orang-utans
Scrabble and screech in the trees.
On beds of moss, I sleep.
In the morning, birds soar above my head.
We feast at night and banquet in the day.
Fruit-covered ivy covers the tree villas.

Orlando Appleby (10)
Irthington Village School, Carlisle

Super Sky

My dog is fast
And I always come last,
My dog is white
And always bites.

My dog is furry as a bear,
My dog is as big as a school,
When I go walking
He likes running.

My dog leaps down the field,
My dog is pale as snow,
My dog eats more than a pig.

Lachlan Ewart (7)
Irthington Village School, Carlisle

My Friends And Family

Bosh is as fluffy as a fluff ball,
When he was little,
He tried to climb the wall.

I have a cat called Chips,
He likes eating apple pips.

Woody and Jesse,
Are very messy.

Bosh likes cats,
But he hates rats.

Chips is fluffy,
He comes home
Wet and scruffy.

Woody and Jesse,
Swim round and round
And also up and down.

None kill,
None will be able
To leave a will.

Oliver Barnes (9)
Irthington Village School, Carlisle

Dogs

They walk on all-fours,
They are furry and soft.
Sometimes they can be as furry
As a fluffy newborn kitten.
Wagging their tails everywhere.

Emma Gallagher (8)
Irthington Village School, Carlisle

My Paradise

The light was glowing like a planet in Heaven
Because it is filmed in Devon
Because the demolisher is Kevin
And he has a Nissan Skyline
The sky is blue, the clouds are as white as paint
And the river, where you can swim all afternoon
Until you have to go to bed
So he said
'Cause you are dead
That is the paradise for me.

Joe Batey (10)
Irthington Village School, Carlisle

Kiara

Kiara is black,
Black as a piece of black paper,
Hyper as a hound dog.
As greedy as a pig!
She chases cats,
She chases rats.
Always chases me!
She scratches me,
She bashes me,
She even nips me!

Rebecca Louise Grice (8)
Irthington Village School, Carlisle

Heaven

Where the angels live,
Where the beasts of old are,
You'll find God there,
Maybe someday you too will go there.

But if you don't,
Who knows where you will end up?

Heaven is a very strange place,
Everyone that goes to Heaven,
Always can do whatever they want,
Wind up their vocal chords,
So they can sing without being embarrassed.

Swim in the sparkling blue lakes,
Now they have those 'all you can eat' bars.

When you open the door to Heaven,
Your friends will be there,
Maybe five, six or seven.

When you look down from Heaven on high,
Ants on wheels whistle by.

Nina Russell (10)
Irthington Village School, Carlisle

Guess?

Walk on all-fours,
Guess how many paws?
You keep them as pets,
Take them to the vets.

They can be as small as mice,
Or as big as a boulder.

Some eat a little,
Some eat a lot,
Cat or dog?
Wart or hog?

Ellen Hill (7)
Irthington Village School, Carlisle

The Time Train

The passengers board quickly
The wheels start to move slowly
You are out of the station now
You are getting faster and faster.

In 1813 the steam train was out
Huffing and puffing all day and all night
Mr George Stephenson loved his own invention
But no passengers boarded these trains.

In 1825 the steam train was thriving
Passengers boarded its public transport
Mr George Stephenson loved his own invention
Now the public steam train was popular.

In 1879 the electric train was out
Running electronically all day and all night
Mr Werner von Siemens loved his own invention
Now we have the modernised train.

In the 1970s the monorail came out
Running smoothly all day and all night
The invention is brilliant I think
Now the monorail is popular but uncommon.

In 2004 every train is out
All working their way into history
The invention is popular from 1813 until now
Now the train is a popular form of transport.

The passengers board quickly
The wheels start to move slowly
You are out of the station now
You are getting faster and faster.

Philippa Bryant (9)
Irthington Village School, Carlisle

Jesse Gray

J is for as jumpy as a kangaroo
E is for as exciting as a mystery
S is for as silly as me
S is for as sunny as the sun
E is for as excellent as a whale

G is for as gentle as a bunny
R is for as rosy as a rose
A is for as amazing as can be
Y is for yelling like a dolphin.

Amy Greenup (10)
Irthington Village School, Carlisle

My Pet Dog

My pet dog
Was little at first
But she was always
Full of thirst
But now she's one
She does not bite
Although she does enjoy
A fight.

Naomi Grace Guzder (7)
Kingsbury Junior School, Kingsbury

Rally Racing Machines

Buckle up in your racing machines,
Engines revving,
Five, four, three, two, one
And they're off!

Freddie Focus takes the lead,
Round the corner whizzes,
Rotten Rover second place,
Oh no, he almost misses.
Freddie Focus hurtles on,
Along and down the straight,
Rotten Rover's luck is out
And oh! straight through the gate!
The poor cow, is very shocked,
She wasn't wearing armour . . .
The milk yield will be down tonight -
They'll be an angry farmer.
Through the muck and long, wet grass,
The cowpats and the thistles,
Rotten Rover slams reverse
And back on track he whistles.
Freddie Focus storms ahead,
Rover's in pursuit -
The angry farmer's joined the race,
It really looks a hoot!

Group Entry Year 5
Lee McWhirter, Robert Keefe, Ryan Cooper, John Redmond,
Thomas Dixon, Vicki Tunstall (9), Megan Bainbridge (10),
Jake Bell & David Bowman
Kirkby Stephen Primary School, Kirkby Stephen

Halle's Poem

Halle is a dog and she's good at doing tricks,
She is friendly with the children,
Cos she covers them with licks.

She's a furry little puppy
And she likes to *woof* and *bark*
At the moving, rustling rubbish
Which is scattered in the park.

Group Entry Year 4
Jonathan Mells, Elliot O'Connor Ramsey, Sean Winder,
James Birkbeck & Duncan Brunskill (8)
Kirkby Stephen Primary School, Kirkby Stephen

The Last Candle On The Shelf

I'm lonely and old and I'm very cold,
I am so sad no one will buy me
Will they? No.
I am so small,
I wish I was cool
Then people would buy me.
I am so tired, I am burning with rage,
That no one will buy me.
It feels like I'm trapped in a cage.
I wish I was out of this old shop,
I wish people would care for me and light me
But that is just a dream.

Connor Brownfield (9)
Lessness Heath Primary School, Belvedere

I Am The Lounge Candle

I am the lounge candle,
When I'm lit, I can see the owners of me
Cuddling up on the sofa
And when people come over
I feel bright and beautiful all the time.

I am the lounge candle,
I always feel safe and secure
On top of the fireplace
But the downside is my structure
It gets smaller and smaller
Every time I'm left on.

I am the lounge candle,
I always see everything
But sometimes wax drips down my face
And it feels horrible as I melt.

I am the lounge candle.

Ryan Church (9)
Lessness Heath Primary School, Belvedere

The Love Candle

I am a candle, friendly and loving,
People keep me warm and safe,
I just love being a candle,
I'm not afraid, I am so brave,
I do not care if I melt,
I like myself because I can be colourful,
I love being a candle because I'm so pretty
If I burn out, I don't care.

Neelam Sahota (9)
Lessness Heath Primary School, Belvedere

The Church Candle

Colourful candle,
Very lively,
I sit in the church all day long,
With weddings and christenings.

Sometimes I cry wax tears,
Sometimes I feel sleepy,
I am always pleased,
Sometimes I get moved about.

I dazzle brightly,
I get tired easily,
People come over and say how lovely I am,
It hurts when I melt.

The bride and the groom are so lovely,
The bride has a lovely dress,
The groom is dressed nicely,
Then, when it's over, I feel sad.

Grace Sheridan (9)
Lessness Heath Primary School, Belvedere

Wax Tears

It's great to be loved like a sapphire
A candle with love scent and I am so colourful
When I am not used I cry wax tears
When I'm lit I start to rot
Sometimes I feel sleepy.

April Chapman (9)
Lessness Heath Primary School, Belvedere

My Life As A Candle

I'm a lovely candle, tall and slim
With a sight of a curvy twist in my body
I also smell of a rose
And I am as colourful as a beautiful rainbow.
I am a lovely candle.

I have the view of a horrible cupboard
They take no notice of me
As I cry runny wax tears,
I only come out when someone comes round
And when they like to show off.

In the cupboard, it is dark and dull
And also very gloomy
I wish I would come out more often
So people can smell my smell and look at me
And so I make them calm after a hard day at work.

Stacey Tuffin (9)
Lessness Heath Primary School, Belvedere

A Poem Of Peace

I'm the loving candle,
Wax dripping in front of your eyes,
When I'm alight
I bring peace to your heart,
When I'm burning
I bring a lovely smell to you,
I'm the loving candle,
When my owner lights me
I cry wax tears,
I become smaller and smaller,
But smell my lovely smell
That brings love to your heart,
Blow me out,
But I'll still be there for you.

Reece Kidman (9)
Lessness Heath Primary School, Belvedere

A Wedding Candle

I am a wedding candle
I make people calm and peaceful
I see the bride and groom
I'm happy because I smell the flowers.
I see the church bells and the vicar
I hear that lovely wedding music and guests crying
Because of the joy they have in their hearts
But I am small
And concerned about why they don't use me
For Christmas, Easter and christenings.
I have been in the family for generations
Just light me up and you will see
The magical things I could be
As I said, just light me and you will see
And leave the rest to me.

Tosin Taiwo (9)
Lessness Heath Primary School, Belvedere

The Church Candle

I'm a church ornament, I keep people calm,
Burning my flame in my home.
I stay on a table in a boring, old church,
I'm sitting here all on my own.

I get very happy, but sometimes sad,
I watch all the people pour into the church.
I see sad things, which make me cry,
I am always watching them search.

I love being in an old, big church,
It's lovely to see people coming and going.
Every hour at every day in every year,
Hearing the great bell dinging and donging.

Rosie Bayne (10)
Lessness Heath Primary School, Belvedere

The Unwanted Candle

I'm not looked after properly
I am a lonely candle
The last one on the shelf
There is one good thing
About being the last one on the shelf
I never die.

I look all twisted up
It is really uncomfortable
I think I smell really nice
I wish someone would at least look at me
I never get any attention
Everyone thinks I smell horrid

Even next door is coming and complaining
I really wish I had a family
I wish I was loved and cared for
At the end of the week
I'm just going to be chucked away.

Toni-Louise Ciplinski (9)
Lessness Heath Primary School, Belvedere

The Miserable Candle

I'm not looked after well
I'm bored of watching the same TV programme
Over and over again
I'm an old candle
I'm annoyed of only being lit once in a lifetime
Is it because I'm weird or am I dead?
I'm an old candle
I get knocked off my space
Like a block of bricks
I feel as if I'm not welcome in my home
Then there are the insects
That make me feel terrified
But most of all, I feel I'm not loved.

Lucy Taylor-Pease (10)
Lessness Heath Primary School, Belvedere

I'm The Lounge Candle

I can get a really hot headache
I can cry wax tears
I'm lit every Wednesday and on a Sunday
I'm a scented candle sitting in the lounge
I'm sitting on the side near a warm chair
The people I live with move me around
So one time I'm sitting on the side
Now I'm on the television.

I get a much better view sitting up here
I can see a man, two boys, one girl and a lady
I love the family I live with
I get cared for.

Rhiana Hill (9)
Lessness Heath Primary School, Belvedere

The Unlit Candle

A cold body
My body is never lit
I am never warm
I see my friend being taken
I am heartbroken and lonely
I hear beeping and I'm very cold
I want to say, 'Choose me!'
But there is a good part to never being lit
I have a very long life
What am I?

Adam Harris (9)
Lessness Heath Primary School, Belvedere

To Be A Happy Candle

When I am lit
I feel scorching
I cry
I cry wax tear
My wax tears
Slip down my body
As if I had just
Jumped into a
Swimming pool
And got back out again
My view is fab
I look at the TV
And the fields
The fields
Are all different
Colour greens
By the way
I smell nice.

Celine Dinning (9)
Lessness Heath Primary School, Belvedere

The Misplaced One

I was misplaced
I feel sad when people put me in a cupboard
Because my owner has got a better candle than me
I cry melting wax tears that make me smaller
I used to sit on the mantelpiece
But now I am in a dusty cupboard
I miss my old home.

Adam Stacey (9)
Lessness Heath Primary School, Belvedere

Dad!

T hanks for nothing
H eartbroken
A ngry with you
N ever want to know you
K illed my heart
S tupid and selfish

F ailed to come home
O bviously you don't care
R espect, you need to get some

N ever gave us anything
O n your own is where you will stay
T emper flooding through my veins
H ell wouldn't have you
I diot
N o decency
G et out of my life!

Matthew Wishart (11)
Lessness Heath Primary School, Belvedere

The Ornament

I'm a little ornament
Small and round
I only get lit when people come round
I think I should get lit more
I am so beautiful
I like my shape
I like my colour.

Casey Finch (9)
Lessness Heath Primary School, Belvedere

The Candle Of Sadness

I'm left in the shop
Next to a bottle of pop
I always thought
That I would be bought
And taken home
But I'm still alone
I have a funny feeling in my tum
That nobody will come
And buy me.

Holly Sturgeon (9)
Lessness Heath Primary School, Belvedere

The Wax Tears

I am a candle loved like a sapphire
I am a candle with a lovely scent
I am a candle bright and colourful
When I am lit, I get hot and cry wax tears
I feel so wonderful when I am lit.

Jack Taylor (9)
Lessness Heath Primary School, Belvedere

Waxy

I sit on a birthday cake
I hear 'Happy Birthday to you'
That's all I ever hear
I get chucked into a cupboard
Until next year
I see a cupboard door for a year.

Joshua Desmond (9)
Lessness Heath Primary School, Belvedere

Being A Church Candle

I love it when the bride and groom kiss
I'm bored when no one's here
I'm so happy when they do the Communion
This is weird, everyone's putting money in a bag
I'm confused, some people are crying
But it's supposed to be a happy moment
I love it when I'm alight, so bright and warm
But when I'm put out, I'm so dark and cold
Can't they leave me on until the end of my days?

Matthew Lanning (9)
Lessness Heath Primary School, Belvedere

Safari

S ound of the jungle, loud and creepy,
A nteaters eat the ants and bugs.
F orest green as can be with a monkey swinging through the trees,
A ngry tigers fighting in the breeze,
R oar of the lions eating their tea,
 I n the desert with snakes.

All these animals from the jungle and desert.

Frankie Stockford (9)
Moretonhampstead Primary School, Newton Abbot

The Elephant Poem

I am an excellent, extremely enormous elephant.
I am an old hairy monster.
My sister says I'm ugly, but I think I'm beautiful and I'm very amusing,
But beware, I can get very, very aggressive.

Josie Garland (9)
Moretonhampstead Primary School, Newton Abbot

Just Me

C razy, creative, curly,
A mazing, annoying, angry,
R ude, rubbish, risky,
A rtful, athletic, assuring.
    Me.

Cara Grimwade (10)
Moretonhampstead Primary School, Newton Abbot

Hate

Hate is black like dark clouds in the sky
Hate sounds like arguments around me
Hate tastes like hot chillies in your mouth
Hate smells like pepper
Hate looks like something going through your mind
Hate feels like anger going round your body
Hate reminds me of hurting someone.

Hannah Watson (10)
Potters Green School, Coventry

Happiness

Happiness is bright red like roses
Happiness sounds like birds singing
Happiness tastes like melted chocolate
Happiness smells like summer flowers
Happiness looks like all the colours that you can think of
Happiness, it feels like you went on a scary ride at the fair
And you're proud
Happiness reminds you of Bonfire Night.

Shannon Finan (10)
Potters Green School, Coventry

Lunch Time Menu

Hunger is terracotta, a burnt shade of red,
Hunger has a fizzing sensation in your mouth
Which makes your belly grumble!
Hunger looks like a fast-food restaurant
Full of salted chips and burgers smothered in red sauce.
It sounds like people slurping their drinks
And forks and knives scraping their plates!
It smells like ovens burning food while people rush around
Collecting orders from demanding customers.
Hunger reminds me of children
Licking ice creams on the burning beach.

Cheryl Culliford-Whyte (10)
Potters Green School, Coventry

Anger

Anger is steaming red,
It's like blood pouring to your head,
It's noisy and you cannot cope,
It tastes like soap and it smells like petrol,
It reminds me of death and you feel
Stressed!

Amanda Bale (10)
Potters Green School, Coventry

Love In The Air

Love is red like the heart drumming fast
Love sounds like butterfly wings flapping
Love tastes like red strawberries with sugar
Love smells like fire burning away
Love looks like the sun twinkling
Love feels like happiness inside me
Love reminds me of my family.

Megan Morris (10)
Potters Green School, Coventry

Fear

Fear is grey like a rainy cloud,
Fear is eerie like a haunted house,
Fear is sour like a bitter lemon,
Fear calls foe like a ghastly demon.

Fear is smoky like a devil's flame,
Fear is a force that leaves you in shame,
Fear is a feeling that gives you darkness,
Fear is a ghoul, cruel and heartless.

Tamsin Collett-Cox (10)
Potters Green School, Coventry

Love

Love is a dark, warm red like the dazzling red-hot sunshine
Love tastes like big, soft, warm hugs
Love smells like your mum tucking you up in bed
Love feels like running up to your mum after your first day at nursery
Love reminds me of when my little brother was born
And I held him for the first ever time!

Jodie Goodreid (10)
Potters Green School, Coventry

The Love Boat

Love is red like a gentle and soft song
Love is silent like a picture of kiss
Love melts in my mouth like Cadbury chocolate
Love is a sweet smell like roses
Love looks like a crystal swan
Love is smooth and delicate like a butterfly
Love is a never-ending dream.

Iona win Channer (10)
Potters Green School, Coventry

Love

Love is red like a fiery flame
Love is a quiet voice calling a name
Love is a taste, a taste of passion
Love is great in its own loving fashion.

Love is someone that longs for care
Love is someone that's always there
Love is a power, the strongest of all
Love is something that never grows small.

Leah Davies (10)
Potters Green School, Coventry

Happiness

Happiness is the colour blue,
Like the pale blue sky that's here today,
Happiness sounds like laughter too!
Happiness tastes like the candyfloss you eat when you're on holiday,
Happiness smells like freshly picked roses that you water with your
hoses,
Happiness looks like a perfect picture,
Happiness feels like the softest sand in the whole world,
Happiness reminds me of all of the things in this poem!

Jenny Lambert (10)
Potters Green School, Coventry

Sean's Happiness Poem

Happiness is like green like the big fields
It sounds like the rustle of tinfoil
It tastes like a big bag of sweets
It smells like lovely chocolate
It looks like bright red roses
It feels like sticky sweets in a jar
It reminds me of my best friends.

Sean Hague (11)
Potters Green School, Coventry

Love

Love is like a sparkling, rosy-red rose dazzling in the sun.
Love sounds like soft music twirling through the air.
Love tastes like juicy strawberries with cream mixed on top.
Love smells like strawberry and cherry air fresher.
Love looks like red petals falling down from the sky.
Love feels like a silky love heart swaying side to side.
Love reminds me of the peaceful songs that birds sing in the air.

Rosie Marsons (10)
Potters Green School, Coventry

Anger

Anger is the colour red, as red as red can get,
Anger looks like a messy smudge smudged everywhere,
Anger tastes like leaves, leaves with poisonous spots,
Anger smells like foul oil from a petrol station,
Anger sounds like a screech, nails down a blackboard,
Anger makes me feel scared,
Anger reminds me of no peace but disaster, fear and hate.

Megan Judd (11)
Potters Green School, Coventry

Love!

Love is red like a glistening, rosy-red lipstick,
Love sounds like the birds tweeting in the sky peacefully,
Love tastes like sweet cherries and strawberries,
Love smells like the sweet scent from a sparkling rose,
Love feels like you have been granted with the best thing
You could ever possibly wish for,
And all of these remind me of *love!*

Sophie Burgoyne (10)
Potters Green School, Coventry

The Good Feeling

Happiness feels like a cool, calm sky that's blue,
The sound of happiness is quiet like a breezy day.
The taste of happiness is like a bubbly taste
Which pops in your mouth,
Happiness smells sweet like a tulip swaying on a sunny day.
Happiness is a good feeling
And looks like a child's happy, smiley face.
The texture of a happy feeling in your hands
Is like a warm and joyful touch
Like when someone loves and cares for you.
This happy feeling reminds me of a hot and sunny day
When everyone has as smile on their face
And are enjoying themselves.

Kayleigh Gray (11)
Potters Green School, Coventry

The Hate

Hate is the colour of dark, gloomy and horrid black,
It sounds like snakes hhsssing in your ear,
It tastes like gooey, slimy, slithering guts.
It looks like an evil dark wizard putting a spell on someone,
It smells like poison gas,
Hate feels like a solid rock where you can't fight back,
It reminds you of your worst enemy.

Jack O'Donnell (11)
Potters Green School, Coventry

Fun Is What We Like

Fun is pink like a huge bag of sticky candyfloss.
Fun is noisy like children laughing on the playground.
Fun is sweet like a sweet sensation going on in your head.
Fun is doughnuts, freshly baked today.
Fun is a fairground when everyone has a great time.
Fun is when you snuggle up in bed with your teddy bear.
Fun reminds me of friendship and love.

Rebecca Oughton (10)
Potters Green School, Coventry

The Power Of Love

Love is red like a fierce, everlasting flame burning in your heart,
Love is quiet like a sleeping baby in your arms,
Love is sweet like a sugar-coated strawberry,
Love is beautiful like a deep red rose,
Love is soft like a lump of cotton wool,
Love is fragile and could be broken in a flash,
Love is something you don't do for cash,
And last of all, something I think is true,
Love is more powerful than me or you.

Demi-Lee Woods (10)
Potters Green School, Coventry

The World

The world is full of many things
From birds to bees
And flowers to springs
If you open your eyes
And look around
You will see
That the world is like
A wonderful sound.

Jamie-Lisa Acton (10)
Potters Green School, Coventry

Love

Love is red like exploding volcanoes
Love feels like a flaming hot boy
Love reminds me of a big bunch of hearts
Love sounds like a heart beat
Love tastes like a big bunch of happiness
Love looks like a big heart
Love smells like a big bunch of roses.

Charlotte Tyrrell (10)
Potters Green School, Coventry

Fear

Fear is black like the darkness of the night,
It sounds like somebody screaming in your ear,
It tastes like something sour and spicy that burns your mouth,
It smells like danger is near,
It looks like darkness and feels like your heart is being ripped out,
It reminds me of your worst nightmare.

Megan Mitchell (10)
Potters Green School, Coventry

At The Stables

Stables are a magical place
A foal has such a beautiful face.
Watching our pony gracefully leap
It's good to have a horse to keep.
Bringing out their saddle and tack
Waiting for a summer's hack.
At the end of the day your horse goes to bed
And rests its little horsy head.

Sophie Gill (11)
Robert Ferguson Primary School, Carlisle

Seasons

Autumn
Autumn time, the leaves are falling
My mum said, 'Hurry up, I've been calling.'
The autumn leaves just go *crunch*
It's time to have school dinners not packed lunch.

Winter
Wintertime is just the best
My Christmas tree is better than the rest
The snow thick and white
It's cold and dark every night.

Spring
Springtime, the sun wakes bright and early morn
Baby lambs are just newborn
Daffodils have just started to grow
But bluebells stay very low.

Summer
Summertime is very hot
My hair gets tied in real knots
Yeah! we've finished school
I can play in the cool pool.

Cara Forrester (11)
Robert Ferguson Primary School, Carlisle

The Gingerbread Man

The gingerbread man was baked one day
He met a horse who liked eating hay.
He met a dog with two paws,
And a fox of course.

The fox liked the taste of gingerbread
This story's gone wrong, he likes chocolate instead.
That altogether is a different story,
It might even get a little bit gory.

Joby Hodnett (10)
Robert Ferguson Primary School, Carlisle

Seasons

Spring
Spring is the start of blue-skied days.
The sun is coming out, having its ways.

Summer
In summer, of course, the sun will be out,
There is no snow or rain about.

Autumn
All the leaves are starting to fall,
Into the pile of leaves I kick my ball.

Winter
The snow is coming from the sky,
To the sun I say goodbye.

Emily Graham (10)
Robert Ferguson Primary School, Carlisle

A Stormy Night

Tonight's a very stormy night,
The rain is splattering off my window,
No dogs or wolves are in my sight,
Yet I hear continuous howls.

The wind is blowing,
It is rustling the leaves of a tree,
I can see the shadow showing,
I can see the full moon.

The thunder and lightning is showing against the black,
I know I'm safe,
Yet it is filling me with fear as branches crack,
When will this storm end?

Katherine Bolton (10)
Robert Ferguson Primary School, Carlisle

Red

Red is a Manchester United top
When they score goals.

Red is a North Bank top
You see them win games.

Red is an Arsenal top
Like Ljungberg's red hair.

Red is a football
In a park.

Red is a pen
Which you colour with.

Red is a wall
In a bedroom.

Thomas McMann (11)
Robert Ferguson Primary School, Carlisle

Boring Sunday

Sunday is boring
Nowhere to go
Nothing to do
I wish I had my friends and co.

Sunday is boring
I think they should
Show more motor racing
Then TV is good.

Steven Atkinson (11)
Robert Ferguson Primary School, Carlisle

Seasons

Autumn the leaves are falling,
The cold nights are calling.
Leaves are on the floor all crispy and brown
People going on autumn holidays out of town.

Winter, it's cold, chilly, freezing at night
Keep hold of your duvet, sleep tight.
The snow is here
Have no fear.

Spring summer days are coming
I can hear the birds are humming.
No more winter nights
Turn off the Christmas lights.

Summer, finally I'm off school
I'll go swimming in a pool.
People trying to get a tan
Gosh! they'll need to get a fan.

Nicole Kidd (10)
Robert Ferguson Primary School, Carlisle

Puppies

I love puppies
Big and small
Puppies, puppies
Great and tall
Puppies, puppies
The best of all.

Jamie Little (10)
Robert Ferguson Primary School, Carlisle

Seasons

Autumn is when the leaves start falling
The mess of the leaves are just appalling
The trees are bare
With no leaves there.

Winter is when you have loads of fun
Playing in the snow and not the sun
The snow goes all around
It's very slippery on the ground.

Spring is when the daffodils start growing
They pop up and start showing
Animals rise early in the morn
Cute, baby lambs start being born.

Summer is when we are not at school
Playing about, splashing in a pool
The sun comes out
Children start to scream and shout.

Chloe Bell (10)
Robert Ferguson Primary School, Carlisle

Perfect Purple

P urple reminds me of my room
   Because it's purple
U se purple felt to colour in pictures
   You can buy them at shops
R eally beautiful colour
   You can get dark and light purple too
P urple is my favourite colour
   You can find purple clothes in shops
L ilac is a lovely colour too
   But I must admit purple is the best
E ver beautiful, never changing
   You just can't change my mind, purple is the best.

Deborah Harrop (11)
Robert Ferguson Primary School, Carlisle

Red Rooney

Red is Rooney
Scoring a goal.

Red is Man U's
Home shirt.

Red is a fire
Giving me warmth.

Red is my Champions
League ball.

Red is the sun
Warming up the sky.

Red is Man U's
Spectators.

All of this makes
The Roon machine.

Adam Ramdin (10)
Robert Ferguson Primary School, Carlisle

Dogs

Dogs are big and small,
Great Danes are very tall.
Labradors, Collies and Greyhounds,
All dogs make a noisy sound.
Dalmatians are my best,
Way ahead compared to the rest.
There are many thousands of dogs,
Lots can jump over logs.

Anthony Heugh (10)
Robert Ferguson Primary School, Carlisle

Seasons

Autumn
Autumn is when the leaves start to fall
I get my sweeping brush and put them in a pile
I take all the leaves to a black bag
Autumn is when the leaves start to fall.

Winter
Winter is when the snow starts to fall
I make loads of snowmen in my garden
I have snowball fights with my friends
Winter is when the snow starts to fall.

Spring
Spring is when the lambs are born
And new flowers start to grow
It starts to get warm in spring
Spring is when the lambs are born.

Summer
Summer is when the hot days come
And I swim in my pool
I get a suntan in the garden
Summer is when the hot days come.

Lauren Lewis (10)
Robert Ferguson Primary School, Carlisle

Babies

My little sister cries all day
My baby brother does the same
Some days it makes me insane
But apart from that it's not that bad
As long as I don't have to change them!

Natasha Isaacs (11)
Robert Ferguson Primary School, Carlisle

Cinderella

Cinderella the poor slave,
Serves her sisters every day.
One day there was a letter,
Her life had got better!
There was to be a great ball,
She finds out she can't go at all!
The sisters are far too slow,
Why on earth do they get to go?
So here it is, the big day,
Cinders will go, she'll find a way.
All day long the ugly sisters,
Sit picking their scabs and blisters.
So at midnight she goes to the ball
And she decides to bomb it all.
So Cinderella the poor slave
Lives in a cell for the rest of her days.

Lucy Maxwell (10)
Robert Ferguson Primary School, Carlisle

Happy Hippos

Down by the jungle where nobody goes,
There's a big fat hippo wearing clothes.
A pink glittered top and red high heels,
She goes up town for so many meals.
Her name is Dawn, she lives with ants,
They like to crawl up her red pants.
Her boyfriend Frank, who's dressed in a suit,
Have you ever seen his lost black boot?
Sarah has it in her room,
Frank can't get in, it's the room of *doom!*
Frank and Dawn then got married,
They went away in a horse and carriage!

Jodie Liddell (10)
Robert Ferguson Primary School, Carlisle

Yellow

Yellow are bananas
Ready to be eaten.

Yellow is my mum's hair
Shining brightly.

Yellow are my books
To write and draw in.

Yellow are the stars
Shining in the night.

Yellow are the daisies
Brightening up the garden.

Yellow is my cup
To drink out of.

Hollie Smith (10)
Robert Ferguson Primary School, Carlisle

All About My Family

When I wake up in the morning
My mam and dad are always snoring
My sister is always watching TV
And never takes any notice of me
My sister likes to cook,
And always seems to be reading a book
Me and my dad take the dog for a walk
And we always have a really good talk.

Adam Gill (10)
Robert Ferguson Primary School, Carlisle

A Silly Spell

Get a cauldron.

Ingredients:
> An apple pie
> A fat spider
> 10 litres of Coke
> One pound coin
> An engine of a motorbike
> An Egyptian pyramid
> 500 books

Finally:
> Put it all in a steel tank
> When you open the tank
> You will get 10,000 pounds.

Nathan Thompson (10)
Robert Ferguson Primary School, Carlisle

Hallowe'en

H allowe'en is the best day of the year (except for Christmas).
A ll the scary witches and warlocks come out to play.
L ittle lanterns shine so brightly.
L ittle children get a fright.
O range pumpkin pie, yum-yum!
W erewolves howl at the full moon.
E erie cries from the black forest.
E ven though I'm 10 years old I'm still dressing up.
N ever shall I miss a night of Hallowe'en.

Amber Jenkins (10)
Robert Ferguson Primary School, Carlisle

Winter

Snow falling day and night
Hailstones give me a fright
Make a snowman
With a carrot for his nose.

Snow as soft as dough
Snowmen flying everywhere
Some falling from the air
It's the end of winter.

Andrew Bell (10)
Robert Ferguson Primary School, Carlisle

Cars

Cars are made in different sizes,
They go to car shows to win their prizes,
My favourite car is a Lotus Spider,
Their road to success is getting wider and wider.
Cars are modified to look really good,
The massive engine is under the hood,
You can get your windows in another shade,
In a car shop is where they are made.

Jordan Cannon (10)
Robert Ferguson Primary School, Carlisle

Sunday

Sundays is when my mam makes nice dinners.
Sunday is when my team plays football and we are the winners.
Sunday is when there is nothing on telly.
Sunday is when there are sweets in my belly.

Tom Townsend (11)
Robert Ferguson Primary School, Carlisle

Tiger

The grass scuttles and sways in the cool breeze of South Africa.
Something moves:
A glow of orange and black comes into view.
His eyes pass me across the waterhole
To a gazelle grazing there -
She hasn't noticed.

Squinting, concentrating, the striped cat slowly pads,
Ready for the catch.
Meanwhile, the gazelle, lapping at her refreshing drink.
Tiger trying to focus;
The gazelle starts to panic. Everywhere is intense.
Claws, teeth and ears are bared -
Pounce!
Blood streams everywhere.
Gazelle -
Dead.

Swiftly padding amongst the luscious green grasses,
Now drenched in blood.
Hanging
From its canine clenchers,
The nest straight ahead, a pine tree
Covered in tiny little orange and black pieces of fur.
He was home.

Olivia Lynch-Kelly (9)
St Peter's RC Primary School, Hinckley

A Fish

Worrying amongst the seas,
George the clownfish was being chased
By a tooth-bloody shark named Nothing!
George's fin was pushing every other clownfish out of the way.
When in a flashback,
A typhoon in the middle of the salty seas appeared.
He was trapped!

The tooth-bloody shark came swooping, swooping.
When in a sudden movement
The typhoon stopped.
He went through and what?
A whole army of sharks!
Sharks came closer, closer.
The other clownfish found prey at the other side.
The sky turned red like some rosy cheeks.

There was a hint of sparkle in the sky,
Hopefully good luck for George
On his journey through the swarm of sharks.
A drop from George's eyes leaked down his cheek.
The other clownfish came to help.
Other clownfish came to help.
Other clownfish came to help.
Thankfully George got away without their help.

Tom Clarke (9)
St Peter's RC Primary School, Hinckley

The Bat Hunting

Swooping in the night,
Millions of them,
Poisoning the area by the second,
But oh, a little rat -
Slam!
It drops to the ground in a flicker of light,
Thousands of bats covering the wretched thing,
With fangs the size of an elephant's trunk.

Squelching them,
Inside and out,
Nothing but guts and bones.
They fly around searching for pure blood from a ratty rat!
Then, in a flash of light,
One bat senses a rat hole.
Taking the risk to the highest level,
The bats fly in and drain all the blood from every rat in the nest!

Mission accomplished for the bats.
They fly home,
Full of blood to keep them alive.

Joseph Langham (10)
St Peter's RC Primary School, Hinckley

Falcon

Nearer, nearer the big, rugged ball of fluffy feathers was swooping
Down and down.
Cute chicks were everywhere in nests.
The falcon was after them, its dinner was ahead . . .
Eap, eap, eap!
The beautiful golden eagle
Whooshed down and hit the falcon flying.
Brer, brer, brer?
The falcon flew away
The rugged eagle had gone.
The golden eagle flew off as well.
The fluffy, golden, cute chicks were in their nests, *asleep!*

David Partridge (9)
St Peter's RC Primary School, Hinckley

Wolf

Its legs as fast as a jaguar,
Getting smaller and smaller.
Turning around to me on the crunching leaves.
Orange, red, brown.
Suddenly it turns again,
After a little mouse.
Running, running after its prey.

Mouse running
As fast as he could.
'Eek!'
'Eek!'
Climbing up a tree
To the very top.
Wolf tries to climb.
It falls and lands in a thorn bush.

Blood dripping
Everywhere.
The mouse returns to its nest
With the wolf's heart.

Emily-Jayne Stanier (9)
St Peter's RC Primary School, Hinckley

Shark

The swoosh of water up and down.
It's trying to get something to eat.
It goes up and
Everyone sees the shark fin.
They all run from it.

It heads for the child who doesn't know
And *bang!*
He chucks him about and he dies!

Declan Rollings (9)
St Peter's RC Primary School, Hinckley

The Wolf

In a deep
Dark street.
I went to the window.
I could see a fierce thing.
I thought it was wolf.
No.
It had shining teeth,
With big, long, sharp claws,
With a golden eye.
Next it spotted me
And *boom!*
It was in my face.
It was a wolf, a fierce one.
I stood back,
Realised it wasn't
After me.
It was after
A little, innocent
Pink mouse.
Bang!
The next thing
I saw was
Fur from the pink mouse.

Shannon Grant (9)
St Peter's RC Primary School, Hinckley

Panting In The Breeze

Panting in the breeze, its shark fins twirling around.
I hear some hooves and wings gather speed,
And dust swarming in on me.
Its eyes are gleaming bright as the dusty moon.
The golden-white waves in the breeze.
It pads a few fearless steps out
On the sandy bush-earth.
But there is an animal that hasn't noticed,
Grazing on a small patch of grass.
Frantically I look around for some cover,
But the dingo has already noticed
And its movement starts to change.

Slowly and carefully, the dingo reveals its claws.
Suddenly the padding stops.
Then, an ear-splitting scrape and hooves shuffle,
But it is too late.
The dingo starts running, leaping,
But he still can't catch up.

Pounding of hooves, scratching of claws,
Swooshes of tails, growling of mouth.
A last blink comes from the buffalo and a pant begins to sigh.
The buffalo bleeds.
As the lava streams down, the dingo howls to attention.
Slowly, carefully drags its limp prey
Back into the sandy desert and starts
Panting
In the breeze.

Aisling Lynch-Kelly (9)
St Peter's RC Primary School, Hinckley

Padding, Roaring, Leaping

Padding, roaring, leaping, running around in the great red sun
Searching for prey, the only panda in these parts.
There was silence in the dark Zhang Forest in the heart of China.
Brushing bamboo and leaves away . . .
But now still,
It was staring directly at me.
Slowly, so very slowly
His eyes turned back to poor young red panda.
Quicker, quicker and then stopped,
As if satisfied that it was close enough.

Then *rooooaar*, but I shouted out.
Slashing, fighting both climbing up trees.
The gleaming green eyes of the tiger,
Its twitching nose,
Its drooling mouth,
The red panda's small black eyes,
Its second thumb drooping.
It jumped below the tiger, as he was jumping.
Chomp!
Caught in the tiger's teeth.

Padding, roaring, leaping,
Running around in the enormous white moon,
Shimmering in the sky,
No longer searching.
Once again silence fell around the forest.
And then it got smaller as it padded down to its family.

Patrick Brown (9)
St Peter's RC Primary School, Hinckley

Bird

Flying amongst the open fields,
There was a beautiful, swooping, glistening bird.
Suddenly, a worm.
The worm saw the leather-protected bird and tried to get underground.

Scampering, wiggling, but too late,
It had it.
The worm had gone.
The poor worm.

The bird started to fly into the sky,
The chicks were waiting, waiting,
Waiting for the lovely, juicy worm.

Zoom, zoom, zoom,
Through the warm, cosy air,
The mummy bird came.
The chicks started to wiggle about and fight.
Splat!
The worm was gulped down one of the chick's throats.

Suddenly, another worm hopped up,
Popped out of the soil,
Along with a load more, looking up, down, left, right.
The fluttering, feathered bird didn't get it.
Why was this happening?

The bird realised that she had killed the Queen Worm.
Then, the King Worm was eaten too.
And all other worms started to be gulped up.

The mummy called for the father bird.

Suddenly, the father bird appeared.
But luckily, father bird didn't have his dinner yet,
But - *gobble, gobble, gobble*. All gone.

And then father bird flew away
And went back to work.

Jessica Tallis (9)
St Peter's RC Primary School, Hinckley

The Great Fish Swims

Gliding, gliding, gently, gently.
Through the deep, dark and foamy oceans.
The gigantic fish swims.
Swish, swish,
Goes the great fish's scaly tail.
Its sharp eye scanning the water for its appetising meal.
It swims willingly, hungrily, silently, snake-like.
Closer and closer, the bloodthirsty vampire comes.
Searching, searching, wide jaws snapping violently and then . . .

There it was.
A helpless school of tiny fish.
The main meal of the day.
The predator strikes.
Whoosh, snap, crunch, gone!
The small fishes disappear into the body of the
Great
White
Shark.
The blood-red tears of each tiny fish come streaming.
The flowing river of death fills the ocean with
The sad story of the aggressive hunt.

From the swift killing the great fish slows down.
Gliding, gliding, gently, gently,
The great fish swims.
Smaller, smaller, blurry, blurry.
Until,
It disappears into the deep blue.
Back where it came from, satisfied with the delicious meal.

Charlotte Ferguson (9)
St Peter's RC Primary School, Hinckley

The Lion Hunt

A roar came from the thick trees.
It could only mean one thing.
It was a lion, padding in the sizzling suns of Africa.
I could see it clearer than ever now
Glistening mysteriously without a shadow.
The lion could hear a quiet bellow from a zebra.
He could see his dinner.

Creeping towards them along the blades of grass.
No noise coming from this huge creature.
I could see the lion thinking to himself,
Should I or shouldn't I?
I could see the lion getting closer to the ground.
Suddenly the lion pounced next to the terrified victim.
The zebra started running for dear life.
The lion caught up with the zebra and slashed its neck
And the red-hot lava came oozing out.
Lion 1 Zebra 0.

The zebra was dead as a dodo.
The lion looked quite pleased with himself.
The lion returned to his children.
I could see the other zebras weeping with fear
Thinking that they could be next.
Smaller
    And
        Smaller until it became completely invisible.

Charlie Smith (9)
St Peter's RC Primary School, Hinckley

Tiger Shark

Gliding swiftly. Speeding through open sea.
Quietly preaching to his prey.
Something jumping wildly.
The prey scatters away.
The creature screeches though the predator circling around.
While the killer thinks it's fresh shark-bait at his door
Like surveillance cameras watching its every move.
The dolphin fiercely smashing the waves in its wild movement.
The shark, like lightning with powerful strokes,
Forward, backwards, up, down.
On its last jump . . .
Smash! Clatter! Crackle!
Round, round - twizzling while crunching the poor fish
With millions of razor-sharp blades.
Then turning, it leaves just bones.

Bethan Kate Fagan (9)
St Peter's RC Primary School, Hinckley

The Fox

A fox was crouching through the trees and woods
Looking for something to eat,
Looking up,
Down, in the trees,
Looking left, right and through the trees.

As the fox was still going to look,
A boy - Cameron -
Limped down from the tree
And killed the fox.
The boy looked for more.
Another fox was on top of the hill,
Howling.
Aoowww! Aooww! Aoowww!
Warning the others of the danger of the little boy.

Leah Axon (9)
St Peter's RC Primary School, Hinckley

The Lion

Padding proudly along through the blazing heat of Africa
Roaring at the animals around him
Then starts to creep around
A group of antelope,
It picks its prey ready for the leap.

Its claws dig into the sand, then silence.
Suddenly it leaps - the group runs
Like there's no tomorrow.
Fortunately it grabs its prey -
All ten claws in its skin.
'Eeeee!' The antelope's helpless.
The lions starts to rip and tear, rip and tear the antelope's body,
The beast's eyes glistening in the blazing sun -
The lion looking very pleased.
Scream! Roar! Scream! Roar!
The antelope lies dead.
After the feast all that was left was blood and bone,
Blood and bone.

The lion padded with blood all over him -
He saw his cubs and they came padding to him.

Jake Hounslea (9)
St Peter's RC Primary School, Hinckley

The Falcon

'Erk, erk!' A small dot is enclosing on something around me.
Sharp beak, clasping claws, expert eye.
Suddenly a squeak,
The bird swerves left, then right.
There was a long silence.
Suddenly the bird swerves above me.
I can see the small rodent being carried off into the horizon.
There was a loud squeak, the heartbeat stops.
The blood-red tears rolled off the mouse.
The falcon flutters off to find more food for its family.

Angus Daly (9)
St Peter's RC Primary School, Hinckley

Eagle

All was quiet:
Protected under the black velvet sky.
Everything was dark,
Except for the white luminous face, a lady's face,
And her jewels are all the stars.
It was warm for night
And the crickets were bleeping
In the lush green grasses of the African fields.
All fell still.
The two totally concentrated eyes of individual sparks,
Looked clever and sly,
Reading across them,
Evil, in every gleaming glint of light;
Claws reflecting light of hunger,
It swooped down on an aim of prey.

Beak fixed, like a drawn sword,
Scuttling through the innocent clouds,
Getting lower and more concentrated
On the scuttling creature on Earth.
Its claws a cage of death, waiting to enclose on its prey.
Out of breath,
Running, scuttling on its needle-sharp legs,
Every swooping bit of air, like a weight on its back.
Breathing its last words of *tarantula. Snatch!*
The river of blood-red liquid poured through the crying rainforest.

Casually back now, its beak no longer a spear,
Its claws clenching the pile of hell: a spider.
Ascending, it swooped, eyes full of excitement,
Beak not weeping from hunger anymore,
Its eyes scuttled in their sockets.
Wings gliding, smaller and smaller; off it went.
Safe, sound, all was protected under the indigo sky.
The sun rose up.
Dawn.

Katharine Lynch-Kelly (9)
St Peter's RC Primary School, Hinckley

The Cheetah

Purring like a cat but looks bigger,
Fast, but cute and cuddly as a teddy bear,
Spotty as a giraffe and claws like knives.
Slowly moving around the jungle in the centre of South Africa,
Trying to find water to gulp down quickly,
Looking for its prey and hot sweat dripping from its mouth.

Soon as it finds its prey,
It slowly moved towards the little blue-eyed bird moving,
Moving nearer and nearer then,
Whoosh!
It jumped and snatched the little bird off the ground,
Then it eats its lunch.

Around the jungle it runs,
But never to reveal its face
As a branch,
Smashes it in,
Its face,
But it has revealed its face,
Then it hides and it promises itself
Never to return to the jungle again.

William Byrne (9)
St Peter's RC Primary School, Hinckley

Pigeon

I saw it.
Beak like a mountain top,
Claws as sharp as you'll ever see,
It pushed its head back and forth,
And waddled, like a duck.
It saw its prey, its prey was a delicious birdseed,
Which a nearby human had thrown.
It couldn't run, of course, or even move,
But the way it chomped, so willingly, like a tiger,
At a nearby victim, death at your doormat,
An animal Jack the Ripper.
The cracking of the nut sounded like bones,
The skin of the nut like human flesh;
Crumbs, like guts.
Looking like a king at a rave,
The way he drank the water from the puddle,
For it looked like he was drinking a cocktail,
The sun looking like a neon light.
The pigeon, now satisfied, to go back to its family,
On the rooftop of seven Smithy Close.

Andrew King (9)
St Peter's RC Primary School, Hinckley

The Snake

Rustling, rattling through the crisp, crunchy leaves,
The slithering, boneless tube weaves its way
Shining along the secretive grass.
When he spots what he looks at he goes faster,
Faster, faster!
He thinks he's got it
But no!
The snake goes faster, faster
Until he gets the rat.

Then, all that was heard was the blood in his mouth
Dripping, *drip, drip*
Until he drinks it dry.
He goes back home with the rat for his family.

Claire Lester (9)
St Peter's RC Primary School, Hinckley

Fox

Padding amongst the autumn leaves.
The wind tosses the browny, orangey-white tail,
Nose as black as coal.
But there was a rustling sound,
A hop.
The prey saw the predator's gleaming eyes.
Stuck on a spot, couldn't move.
Like it was dead.
Ready to pounce for its tea.
Its ear twinkled and flicked -
Twitch, twitch, flick, flick.
It was ready - *jump, jump!*
Red lava everywhere.
Munch! Munch!
It returned to its hole.

Isobel Swinfield (9)
St Peter's RC Primary School, Hinckley

The Red Squirrel

Scuttling among the fallen brown leaves was a creature,
A small creature,
    A scampering creature,
        An endangered creature.

It was softly,
    Quietly walking along towards the big oak tree,
        Waiting patiently,
            For vibration from movement of human beings.
I quietly walked towards the red,
    Bushy-tailed creature.
Had it seen me?
No! There was a huge bird swooping above,
    That's what it had seen,
    It was darting around, trying to find a hiding place.
    But then, no, it doesn't,
    It's gone into the wide beak of an eagle.
Lying among the fallen brown leaves was a creature,
A small creature,
    An endangered creature,
        A bloodied creature.
The slayer of the dead red squirrel,
    Swooped off,
        Into the snow-white clouds.

Millie Vozza (9)
St Peter's RC Primary School, Hinckley

Shark Attack

Swimming loudly,
Something grey in the big blue.
It's getting louder, louder,
It sounds like it's coming near our boat.
I just see suddenly a big grey tail, sharply pointed.
After waiting, waiting, I think it is all clear.
Suddenly I see the biggest set of teeth ever.
Each and every one pointed and carved,
Like a work of art.
Then straightaway I know what I am dealing with.
Just then, like a whip of light, it goes down,
    down,
       down
Like it is diving to its prey.

Then it comes up to the surface - about 2 metres away
From our boat,
Blood all round its mouth and teeth.
Its eyes gleaming,
It
    waits,
       waits,
For one sudden movement.
Suddenly,
It dips into the hollow sea.

Shadows dawn in as the shark approaches once more.
This time with its prey in its cruel, blood-eating teeth.
It swims, swims in the deep blue with the victim in its teeth.
It swims professionally while glancing at the seaweed
Down below.
And swimming away from the victim,
I see the young shark near an underwater hole.
Fading, fading, swimming away,
Now
    fading,
       fading,
Into the salty seas of death.

Libby Hands (9)
St Peter's RC Primary School, Hinckley

The Creature Of The Woodland Forest

A long, soft, silky tail hanging out of a bush.
A beautiful animal awakes.
I can see the shine on its soft, gentle fur.
Its eyes are green, blue, brown.
But the most beautiful legs padding across the woodland forest.

Then I hear it - *squeak, squeak!*
The fox has found its prey.
A little creature comes running past
Scuttling round my feet.
A sly, fierce creature marching out of its warm, cosy nest.
The fox encloses on me and a
  Scared creature,
  A small creature,
  A scampering creature.

The creature runs away but the fox goes off to its warm home
Where three little soft, beautiful cubs have just fallen asleep.

Lucy Knights (10)
St Peter's RC Primary School, Hinckley

The Hunt

Creaking noise all around,
Growls,
Stumping feet running like a leopard.
Dark fur flashing, gaining on its prey,
Closer and closer,
Faster and faster.

Getting anxious,
One swipe with its claw
And the deer collapses to the ground.
Its red tears land with it
Ripping the flesh, piece by piece.

Returning to its family
With a feast of death.

Andrew Rice (9)
St Peter's RC Primary School, Hinckley

Spider

Looks up, down, sideways,
Looking for its prey,
It's a tarantula.
It's coming quickly,
Faster, faster, still looking for ants.
Juicy, juicy ants.
The spider jumps,
Destroying the ants' nest.
It's wrecking everything.
It's webbing the nest.

Flies coming quickly.
Bang, bang, bang,
The flies are stuck in the web.
Gobble, gobble,
The flies are no more.
Continuing this act till the bees come.
Sting, sting,
The spider cannot take much more
So he makes a web.

The bees break through.
They charge at the spider,
Then the spider dies.

Cameron Miller (9)
St Peter's RC Primary School, Hinckley

The Dark Midnight Garden

Padding softly,
Round the dark midnight garden.
Tail swishing, whiskers twitching,
Nose sniffing.

Squeak, squeak!
Had she heard it in the dark midnight garden?
Scuttle, scuttle!
Had she found it in the dark midnight garden?
Then I saw it,
Blood seeping out, dark, warm tears.

Crunch, crunch!
She was moving, the leaves beneath her paws crackled
In the dark midnight garden.
Squelch, squelch!
Back over the muddy garden, back to her nest.

Katie Pinnock (9)
St Peter's RC Primary School, Hinckley

My Life As A Leaf

I'm a banana leaf in Tanzania,
It's really hot here and I'm very dehydrated.
I'm huge and as green as an emerald,
Soon it will be autumn and I'll be dying away.

It's the first day of autumn and I'm very nervous,
Whoo! Here I go, this way and that.
I land with a crash on the ground.

Big, black hunters break and cut through other leaves like me,
I hear them scream, I'm glad I'm not them.
Whoo! Oh no, they trampled me, now I'm dead
All wrinkled and curled
Rotting away from this wonderful world.

Chloe Loftus (10)
Skelton School, Penrith

My Life As A Leaf

I
am
curled
up as a
bud right now,
it's springtime,
I can feel the warm
sun. I want to get out,
slowly I start. I am a baby
leaf, growing up into a big
leaf, the sun beating down.
It's gone behind a cloud. The
rain has started and the wind
is blowing. I've come off my branch.
The wind is lifting me higher and higher.
This must be what they call autumn. The
season of the dead for all the leaves. The
wind has broken. I'm swirling down all the way
to the ground. Faster and faster I go. Suddenly
I hit the ground with a thump. I am all golden,
I'm glinting in the sun. The rain has started
again. So has the wind. At least I am
sheltered from the rain under the
tree. A hedgehog has dragged
me off. I'm in his nest now.
He is curling up on me.
I am dead now. He has
squeezed the rest
of the life
out of
me.

Madelaine Morfett-Murdock (10)
Skelton School, Penrith

A Leaf's Life

In
the bud
I lie so, so
safe and cosy.
Inside I'm a bit rosy.
But still I'm like in a cot,
nice and hot. I burst free,
still attached to the tree. The
golden sun shone nice and
bright, I looked at the view, what a
height! Soon I broke away into some
hay. Then a bird picked me up
and put me in its nest. I tried
to escape but I did my best.
I looked up, overhead . . .
crush! I'm
dead.

Thomas Bray (10)
Skelton School, Penrith

Leaf

As
Spring
Approached
I was bright green,
cosy as a hedgehog.
Slowly I flowered to a
bright purple then my branch
snapped. I floated to the
damp ground. There
I lay turning
to black
mould.

Joe Jones (9)
Skelton School, Penrith

A Year As A Leaf

I
started
life in a
bud, it was
warm and snug,
then one sunny day
I exploded out, caught
first sunlight, then it started
to rain and hail, the sky turned
a murky grey colour, lightning
struck my twig, I fell to the
ground, faster and faster
I went, I turned autumn
and I turned brown,
a bird took me away,
I ended my year
safe in
a nest.

Harriet Holme (9)
Skelton School, Penrith

Mouse

I hide in holes throughout the day,
But when night falls I want to play,
I sneak around and look for cheese,
So be my friend and help me please.

Becky Atkinson (10)
Skelton School, Penrith

I'm A Golden, Crisp Leaf

I
opened
up from my
bud, the sun
shining bright. My
twig as strong as rope
but when the wind starts to
blow it's not rope anymore,
it's snapped. I twist and turn,
I'm on the ground, I'm being
carried away. Something's
sitting on me, it's a
spiky ball. I think
it's a
hedgehog.

Lee Dixon (10)
Skelton School, Penrith

A Leaf's Life

As
I open
from my bud
I thought I'd fall
into mud. As autumn
approaches I turn all gold
then all cold. I cling on tight
for the fear of flight. But I whirl to
the ground to be found by a bird
that swooped down low.
Then I was taken to a
nest where I could
rest but to have
my sorrow
death.

Cameron McKillop (9)
Skelton School, Penrith

My Life As A Leaf

I started my life high, high up in a tree.
I felt warm and secure.
Even though I was warm and secure
I still felt scared.
I didn't know what would happen in life.
I started growing older and started getting bigger.
My veins are strong, rough and bumpy.
I'm emerald green turning golden brown.
I'm starting to fall,
I'm falling,
I'm floating,
I'm on the floor now.
I'm in a hedgehog's mouth
Being taken to its nest.
I feel cosy and warm,
I'm rotting away now.

Bye . . . bye . . .

Hannah Potts (10)
Skelton School, Penrith

My Leafy Life

When I sit in my cosy home,
Looking round my small dome,
Can't wait to see a little space,
A smile will fall upon my face.

I leap and touch the clear sky,
I feel as if I am to fly,
'*Oh no,* I'm going down,' I said,
'This is not my cosy bed.'

Some more leaves fall on top of me,
I can't think or see, see, see,
Now I'm brown and rotting away,
No one comes out or to play.

The wind blows me into a stream,
Now I'm really clean,
I rot away now,
Off I go . . .

Victoria Baker (9)
Skelton School, Penrith

Leaf Life

Here I am waiting
Waiting till I flower
The sun is hot
It must be soon
A crack in my home,
I become a leaf.
There I am sitting
So bold till the winter
Winter comes I
Depart from my
Branches!
Down I sway
This is the day
That my
Leaf life
Will go!
There I lie
Motionless
Thinking.
Finally I go
With one shred
Of the mower.

Jonathan Pickup (10)
Skelton School, Penrith

My Life As A Leaf

I was safe as a bud,
Warm and cosy
Excited to grow
Waiting for the world to see me.

I am ruby-red, soft and sharp,
But soon I'll be mouldy brown.

Falling off my branch,
Tumbling to the ground,
Nervous, don't know what to do,
Suddenly a bird picks me up,
And flies me to its nest,
I am squashed against a twig.
That
     was
        the
            end
                of
                    my
                        life.

Arabella Stalker (9)
Skelton School, Penrith

Leaf Life

I
Start as
A bud sitting
In mid-air, a green
Oval shape just sitting
There.

I eventually turn into a
Big green oak leaf in the
Air joined to a thin branch.

Suddenly I hear a crack
The branch is falling
Faster and faster
It then goes *bang*
I hit the ground.

Now I'm dead
I just lie
In a heap
Of soil.

Dale Mounsey (9)
Skelton School, Penrith

A Leaf's Life

Here
I am
in my pod
of green on
top of the tree
on a little twig, the
other ones are so big
and mean, they are so tall.
Oh no! It's happening, the dead
wind. I feel light and airy, the
ground is getting closer and
closer and closer, I'm near the
end now, the worms are
eating me. Now I'm
dead in
the
ground.

Sam Blackburn (10)
Skelton School, Penrith

Autumn And Winter

Golden leaves falling from the trees
Open the door, all you can see is leaves
Run towards them
Leaves
Winter's coming
Snowflakes falling from the sky
Flakes
As the sun sparkles on the snow
Flakes
Make the snow look beautiful.

Zoë Eland (8)
Stainton CE Primary School, Penrith

Awesome Autumn To Wonderful Winter

Autumn is the second last season of the year,
Where leaves seem to fall everywhere.
Leaves are floating and twirling,
Next thing they're falling and whirling.
Then the days get much shorter,
The nights get much longer,
The weather gets much colder . . .

. . . And then it's wintertime!
Children see the snow glistening,
Parents just sit there listening.
People stroll through the snow,
Leaving footprints as they go.
With snow on the ground,
There's hardly a sound . . .

Emily Dunn (8)
Stainton CE Primary School, Penrith

Autumn Turns Into Winter

It was autumn and the leaves were fiery.
The children kicked the leaves.
The leaves twirled like a ballerina onto the ground.
The breeze is gusty.
The squirrels are hunting for juicy nuts to eat
For autumn and winter.
The snow and snowflakes come down slowly
Like a bird flying down.
The snow is colder than a fridge.

Deza Thompson (8)
Stainton CE Primary School, Penrith

Autumn Into Winter

On an autumn's day you will see
Conkers on the ground,
Berries in the bushes,
Hedgehogs making beds out of leaves,
Leaves start changing to ruby-red, bronze, golden,
Altogether make a big, fiery coat.
When it is winter the snow makes a blanket,
Crunch, crunch, crunch.
I shiver cos the cool is deafening my ears.
The snow is like pearls in my eyes.
The trees are gleaming with ice and icicles too.

Katie Scott (8)
Stainton CE Primary School, Penrith

Last Seasons Of The Year

Autumn is dry, leaves fall from the trees.
There are scarlet-red, golden or amber,
Falling down from the trees.
Squirrels make footprints in the mud,
They're getting ready for winter.
Autumn has lost his crown,
Autumn has died - no more twirl, twirl, twirl.

Winter is a silver season.
The icicles glisten in the winter sun
Like diamonds or sapphires.

Elizabeth Richardson (8)
Stainton CE Primary School, Penrith

Sunny Autumn To Snowy Winter

Where had all the animals gone?
Like someone set a time bomb.
Everyone just stopped and stared up at the trees,
The sky up there.
Looking at the floor covered with leaves.
All that happens, flows with the breeze.
Look at the snow on the floor,
It almost looks like a blanket once more.
When the snow comes down it whispers
Like little fairies twinkling down.
With the sapphire sky and the white snow.
That's what makes time flow.

Bethany Rouse (8)
Stainton CE Primary School, Penrith

Last Two Seasons

Gusty winds make amber leaves flutter,
Brown squirrels gathering nuts up,
That lay silent on the floor.

Winter, people making snowmen in the frosty snow,
Children beaming with delight that the sparkling snow has come,
Sliding down on sledges which have no brakes,
Winter has come, that's all I can say!

Lewis Pamphilon (8)
Stainton CE Primary School, Penrith

Autumn To Winter

Autumn starts off as a breezy wind
Leaves amber, gold, ruby and bronze,
Fluttering down and end with a crunch,
Big ones, small ones and lots more too,
Everyone having fun in the leaves,
Crunching in them, jumping in them
Playing in them,
Autumn is over,
Winter has come,
No leaves on the trees, all bare,
Just the fir tree has some,
Now the sky is sapphire-blue,
Everyone is shivering,
Sparkling snow is everywhere.

Georgina Fisher (8)
Stainton CE Primary School, Penrith

Sunny Autumn To Snowy Spell Of Winter

All the leaves are on the ground
Squirrels are collecting nuts for winter
Branches are blowing off
Fields are gradually covered in snow
We go sledging on the hills
I play snowball fights
I love it when autumn turns to winter.

Jamie Leah (8)
Stainton CE Primary School, Penrith

Autumn

Autumn, winter
Fiery bronze leaves, crunchy, spinning
Gusty winds chase golden storms of leaves
The children love stamping in the crunchy gold, ruby, scarlet, amber,
bronze leaves

Quick, morning is here, winter is here,
Blanket of silver stuff is covering the Earth,
The sky lilac.
Look down below and you will see the snowflakes dancing on the
snowy floor.

Amy Hullock (8)
Stainton CE Primary School, Penrith

Autumn Changes To Winter

In the time of autumn
The leaves are scattered all over the park.
Golden leaves fluttering from the trees.
First day of winter,
The snow shining upon the floor.
Crunchy snow.
Footprints in the snow
Lead to Stainton School.

Greg Hall (9)
Stainton CE Primary School, Penrith

Autumn Becomes Winter

One Friday ruby-red leaves
Fluttered down and blew across the park.
Then they drifted across the streets.
A month later silver snowflakes fluttered down
And across the park
With all different shapes.
Then they drifted across the street.

Tom Kendal (8)
Stainton CE Primary School, Penrith

Snow Spell

In the park all you can see is golden, ruby and amber leaves.
The slide has leaves on and the swing has too.
It is the end of autumn now
So we are all happy to see winter tomorrow.

Today it is winter, there is snow everywhere.
There are icicles dropping onto the floor.
There is a beautiful rainbow in the sky.
Everyone is running around and playing snowy games.

Holly Foster (8)
Stainton CE Primary School, Penrith

End Of Autumn

Wind starts to blow,
Leaves start swirling,
I thought of people dancing,
Like delicate leaves.

Falling snow from the sky,
Lots of silver snowmen gleaming,
Like huge, crystal statues,
But every second the men are beaming.

Katy Mason (8)
Stainton CE Primary School, Penrith

Autumn Month Into Winter

The summer's gone and autumn's come.
Golden leaves are falling down off the trees.
Winter's here and there's white on the path.
Snowflakes on my window.

James Buck (8)
Stainton CE Primary School, Penrith

A Poem For The Last Seasons

Autumn's here, summer's gone
Don't be sad, autumn's fun
Amber, orange, ruby-red
Leaves for patchwork quilt for bed
Autumn's gone, let's go
Hey, let's go playing in the snow.

Winter's here, time to ski
But first let's have a cup of tea
Silver, icy, freezing snow
Like some frozen pearl - like Play-Doh
Twirling, whirling, icy breeze
No leaves left on the trees.

Lucy Ward (8)
Stainton CE Primary School, Penrith

Untitled

Golden leaves spinning down.
Breezy wind sprinting and sprinting.
Crunchy, crunchy tree leaves.
Shivering down to earth.
World changing.
Snow soft as anything.
Blankets.

Ben Harvey (8)
Stainton CE Primary School, Penrith